Only a Penny

How a Lebanese-American Family Overcame Profound Poverty and Found Prosperity

Sharon Abercia and John Evans

This book is a memoir reflecting the author's present recollections of experiences over time. Its story and its words are the author's alone. Some details and characteristics may be changed, some events may be compressed, and some dialogue may be recreated.

Published by River Grove Books
Austin, TX
www.rivergrovebooks.com

Copyright © 2024 Sharon Abercia and John Evans

All rights reserved.

Thank you for purchasing an authorized edition of this book and for complying with copyright law. No part of this book may be reproduced, stored in a retrieval system, or transmitted by any means, electronic, mechanical, photocopying, recording, or otherwise, without written permission from the copyright holder.

Distributed by River Grove Books

Design and composition by Greenleaf Book Group
Cover design by Greenleaf Book Group

Publisher's Cataloging-in-Publication data is available.

Paperback ISBN: 978-1-63299-879-8

Hardcover ISBN: 978-1-63299-935-1

eBook ISBN: 978-1-63299-880-4

First Edition

I BELIEVE IN YOU

I believe in you, and I believe in your destiny.

I believe that you are contributors to this new civilization.

I believe that you have inherited from your forefathers an ancient dream, a song, a prophecy, which you can proudly lay as a gift of gratitude upon the lap of America.

I believe you can say to the founders of this great nation, "Here I am, a youth, a young tree whose roots were plucked from the hills of Lebanon, yet I am deeply rooted here, and I would be fruitful."

And I believe that you can say to Abraham Lincoln, the blessed, "Jesus of Nazareth touched your lips when you spoke, and guided your hand when you wrote; and I shall uphold all that you have said and all that you have written."

I believe that you can say to Emerson and Whitman and James, "In my veins runs the blood of the poets and wise men of old, and it is my desire to come to you and receive, but I shall not come with empty hands."

I believe that even as your fathers came to this land to produce riches, you were born here to produce riches by intelligence, by labor.

I believe that it is in you to be good citizens.

And what is it to be a good citizen?

It is to acknowledge the other person's rights before asserting your own, but always to be conscious of your own.

It is to be free in word and deed, but it is to know that your freedom is subject to the other person's freedom.

It is to create the useful and the beautiful with your own hands, and to admire what others have created in love and with faith.

It is to produce wealth by labor and only by labor, and to spend less than you have produced that your children may not be dependent on the state for support when you are no more.

It is to stand before the towers of New York and Washington, Chicago and San Francisco saying in your heart, "I am the descendant of a people that builded Damascus, and Byblos, and Tyre and Sidon and Antioch, and now I am here to build with you, and with a will."

You should be proud of being an American, you should also to be proud that your fathers and mothers came from a land upon which God laid His gracious hand and raised His messengers.

Young Americans of Syrian origin, I believe in you.

—Gibran Khalil Gibran

I'D RATHER WALK

I'm sitting at the kitchen table with the newspaper in front of me. Adelene is at our other home on the island, and I'm enjoying a few minutes of quiet after returning from church. It was a beautiful service, and as usual, I loved being there with everyone. But now I'm happy to be home and safe.

The *Houston Chronicle* is the same as always. Nothing really special, but I like reading it anyway. I have to know what's going on in the city and see what my business partners and friends are doing. I like the business and real estate sections, but my favorite is reading our daily political news. How different my country is now from the way it was when I was younger.

Suddenly, I am not enjoying the paper as much as I should. I'm having trouble reading and staying focused. My vision is fuzzy, and, for some reason, my stomach is upset. I spy the bucket of Kentucky Fried Chicken on the kitchen counter and mumble a mild curse at the colonel. He was apparently an ill-tempered businessman; I can't help but think he is reaching out from beyond the grave to give me a good dose of indigestion.

As I look at the front page again, I realize my vision is beginning to narrow. I fear I'm in real trouble now, but I try to talk myself out of it. This has worked for me so often in my life, and I'm hoping it will today, but I'm beginning to have my doubts. Everything starts to go black.

The next thing I know, Ralph Jr. is standing over me, yelling.

"Dad, are you okay? Dad? *Dad!*"

It's like waking from a dream. I'm not sure where I am or what exactly is happening. I tell my son I'm fine. I always have to be strong for my family. I quickly realize I'm not seated anymore. I'm on the floor. I look around and see blood. *Damn, I must be scaring Junior to death.*

He helps me to the chair. I pretend not to need the help.

"I'll be fine in a minute. I just lost my balance."

Ralph looks at me, and says, "You passed out, Dad. Your mouth is bleeding. You are not fine!"

I try to think of something to say to assuage his concern. I want to form a response. Nothing is coming. I'm frustrated now.

"Ralph, please put the phone down!"

Ralph is talking to the 911 operator.

"Stop," I say.

He ignores me.

I raise my voice to get his attention.

"Stop, Ralph. Stop, damn it!"

I think the swear word will get his attention, as I never use them. It's not working. He is still on the phone, so I try to appeal to his tender heart. "I'm fine. Really, I'm fine," I say as calmly as I can.

He looks at me like I'm nuts. I must look pretty bad. While I am wiping my face, I feel a rough, jagged edge against the back of my hand. I realize that when my face hit the floor, I broke a tooth—that's the reason for the blood.

"I'll drive to the hospital. Hand me my car keys." I command, thinking this will appease him, but he won't put the phone down. I tell him again and again, but he persists. He usually listens to me, but not today. I am too tired to argue any further and resign myself to a ride in an ambulance, although I am not looking forward to it. I am also beginning to wonder how I will explain this to my family. I'm sure Ralph Jr. will be calling them soon. He only needs to tell one of them and the phone lines will light up in a matter of seconds.

I don't know why the medics have to take me out on a stretcher. I can walk to the ambulance and step in, but they won't let me—too much liability. Being a lawyer, I should understand. Still, as a man, I'd rather walk under my own power. Being wheeled around makes me feel like one of those World War II 4Fs who were unfit for service. I hate it.

Next thing I know I am in the emergency room. I open my eyes and see the beautiful, loving, concerned faces of my children hovering over me—Sharon, Sandra, Mary Kathryn, and Ralph Jr. Our family doctor, Dr. Ata Salak, walks in.

"Ralph, you need a pacemaker," he announces without even a hello. He shrugs his shoulders and looks for a reaction.

In total shock, I straighten up in my hospital bed.

"A pacemaker? No. No! I just passed out. Maybe I have hypoglycemia. Maybe it's anemia. But not my heart. I don't want or need a pacemaker. That's for old people," I argue.

I have survived cancer three times, but my heart has always been stable.

"Are you sure?" I ask Dr. Salak.

His reply is certain and emphatic.

"Absolutely, Ralph. Your heartbeat is erratic, and the rate is very low. You need a pacemaker immediately."

The room is silent. Everyone is in shock and disbelief thinking, *Not the heart.* Yet we all know that Dr. Salak, a man whom we all respect and love, has a sixth sense when it comes to medicine. He can examine someone and tell right off what is wrong, even before blood work or X-rays. He is a gifted diagnostician, and he is always right. We rely on him without question. He is right this time as well. The EKG reveals that my heart rate *is* erratic, and I *do* need a pacemaker.

I hear the rumble of my four children, who seem to be deciding my fate. They want to move me from the neighborhood hospital down to the medical center. I try to voice my opinion, but they're not listening. Finally, I slap my hand on the bedsheet.

"If I need this done now, let's do it here and quit wasting time," I declare.

A decision is never easy in my family. Everyone is an independent thinker—we were raised to be. Even when the answer is clear, we have to talk it over . . . and over . . . and over. It's the Lebanese way, and it's our family's way.

As I see my children standing in the hospital room, I recall my own youth and our family's meager beginnings. We lived off North Main in those days. It never mattered how much or how little we had; our values never changed. To this very moment, our commitment to God, family, and country has been unwavering. These are the values that were instilled in my sister, my four brothers, and me. They are the same values I've passed on to my children.

I suddenly realize it's been a long journey from our little two-bedroom house at 2005 Freeman Street.

ONLY A PENNY

We were poor—but this does not accurately describe our status. In all honesty, we were desperately poor; we struggled to have enough food to eat and shoes to wear. By the age of seven, I was selling flowers on street corners in downtown Houston at The Rice, formerly the Rice Hotel. Violets grew wild in our tiny backyard. My mother, Libbie, was so talented. She picked the flowers, wrapped them with colored twine, and made beautiful bouquets. I would take her handmade creations, place them oh-so-carefully in the carton she had prepared with beautiful linen, and make my way downtown to wait outside the big hotels and restaurants. As the fancy couples strolled by, I offered bouquets to the men wearing their expensive suits. I would nod my head, wink, and say, "Flowers for your lady, sir?"

This simple line proved to be an effective sales ploy and often got me a pinch on the cheek.

"Oh, honey! He is so cute!" the ladies would say.

I never failed to sell all the flowers I had.

As the seasons changed and the spring blooms wilted, I had to find other things to sell. Sometimes I sold my mother's delicious bread; other times, I used my talent for making shoe leather look as shiny as a mirror.

On one occasion, my uncle, who was actually nine months younger, asked to accompany me and help sell my wares. I know having a younger uncle sounds strange, but my mother married early and had me at only sixteen. Her mother, Annie, had William, the last of eight children, just before she turned forty. Everyone had big families back then, and everyone married young.

Even though William was younger than me, I always called him Uncle William. Even when we were children, I made sure to give him the respect he deserved. In return, Uncle William taught me how to buy low and sell high. He was a natural wheeler-dealer, even at the tender age of six. I learned everything from him.

We would walk several miles to Produce Row and buy an apple for a penny. Then, we would head downtown and sneak up the stairwell of the local department store to sell our apple. Two cents was our price. With our newfound profits, we would scurry back to Produce Row and buy two apples this time. The miles seemed like blocks then. When I look back at how far we walked each day, I am in awe.

Saturday was always a good day for selling apples. We had the whole day, no school, and the department stores were filled with shoppers and employees. We purchased the biggest, most delicious red apples—ones that made your mouth water. Uncle William and I would climb the stairs to the top floor of Foley Brothers and hide in the stairwell so the security guards would not see us. As shoppers walked from floor to floor, we caught their eyes by nodding our heads. Then, we presented our apples.

The employees were our best customers; however, to sell to

them, we had to be brave and go onto the floor where they worked. We would run onto the floor, sell our apples as fast as we could, and then run back to the stairwell. If the guards caught us, they would throw us out and kick us down the street with vengeance.

I remember the first time I sold ten apples in one day—I thought I had struck gold. Twenty cents for a day's work was incredible!

One Saturday morning as we were headed out to sell apples, Uncle William exclaimed, "Let's go meet the mayor!"

I looked at him as if he had lost his mind.

"You don't know the mayor," I said.

"I know, but that's not going to stop us. Follow me. He will see us."

We walked to City Hall and flew up two flights of stairs to the mayor's office.

"Hello. How can I help you?" his secretary greeted us cordially.

"As citizens, we have come to see the mayor," Uncle William announced.

She looked at us and smiled.

"You have? What business do you have with the mayor?"

I saw Uncle William's mind working before he blurted out.

"We have come to sell him an apple. We know these are his favorite."

She laughed, picked up the phone, and had a quiet conversation. She then turned back to us.

"The mayor will be happy to see you young men. Please go right in," she said.

The mayor, Oscar Holcombe, was a very distinguished, white-haired man. He stood as we entered and invited us to sit. He asked for our names and inquired about what we were doing on a Saturday. We told him we were selling apples to help our family. We talked for a few more moments; he listened politely while he inspected us from head to toe.

When we finished, he asked, "Are these the only pair of shoes you boys own?"

He had obviously seen the holes in the bottom of our shoes.

"Yes, sir, they are," we answered at the same time.

Mayor Holcombe called his secretary into his office and instructed her take us to Connor's Shoe Store for a brand-new pair. He also bought an apple from us. I couldn't believe our luck. Uncle William and I had met the mayor of Houston, sold him an apple, and gotten a new pair of shoes on top of it all.

Once I learned the skill of selling from Uncle William and knew my way around town, I asked my younger brother Johnnie to join us. Uncle William and I were close, but no one was as close to me as Johnnie. We were brothers and best friends until the day he died. We were the oldest boys, only eighteen months apart. The burdens of our family fell on our shoulders, but we never complained. We did everything together: we sold papers, shined shoes, played baseball, had rock fights with the neighbors, double-dated, served in World War II, and even ended up in the same profession as adults. We had a bond like no other.

We called ourselves the "Three Musketeers." The first thing Johnnie sold with Uncle William and me was the *Houston Chronicle*. We would buy two papers for three cents total, and then sell them for three cents each. Uncle William and I would go all over downtown selling papers, but Johnnie stuck to the corner of Texas and Travis, next to the Milby Hotel and Walgreens. He

Wednesday, November 6, 1957 — Section C, Page 9

BOY BEFRIENDED BY MAYOR IN '33 MAY SERVE WITH HIM

It was a frigid February day in 1933 when the mayor of Houston spotted his newspaper delivery boy making the City Hall rounds barefoot.

He sent his secretary with the boy to buy him a pair of shoes.

Time passed, and the youngster grew into manhood. He worked and studied, passed the bar and joined the ranks of Houston's attorneys. He never forgot the kindliness of the city's top executive.

Now the attorney—Ralph Abercia—is making his first political race, seeking election as councilman from District A.

If elected, he may serve with the man who bought him the shoes that cold February day, Mayor Oscar Holcombe.

Now! A Super Tablet for Relief of Arthritis-Rheuma...

Not a "Temporary Relief Pill."
Pain Relief*— Eve...

NEW YORK, N. Y. (Specia...
Doctors at three leading ar...
clinics reported that a rem...
new medication gives s...
relief from a...
...atism p...

Houston Chronicle article about Ralph getting his first pair of shoes from Mayor Holcombe.

would not budge. I would beg him to follow us, but I can still see him with those big dark eyes and thick black hair, all of six years old, shaking his head.

"This is my corner, and I am not going to lose it," he would say. He was smart—the newspaper press was just behind him. Everyone knew it was Johnnie's corner.

If selling the evening edition was the work that made up our salaries, selling extras was how we made our bonuses. I don't even remember how we found out there were extras to sell. We somehow just knew and would show up at the newspaper loading dock. There was always a crowd of us kids there, and we would jockey to be at the front of the line. After all, the first kid on the street with an extra was sure to sell out. I would get my stack, tuck the papers under my arm, and run down the street yelling—yes, you've got it—"Extra, Extra, read all about it!" Everyone did. After all, that's how the world got its news back then. There were no computers or iPhones. There was no Internet.

I'm sure it sounds odd now, but I still like getting the news from a physical paper. There is something so comforting about the feel of newsprint between my fingers. The sound, the smell, and the quality of the journalism were so much better back then. Or maybe that's just the way I remember it. I also liked the interaction. We don't get much personal interaction with a computer or the Internet. But when I was on the street with an extra in my hand, people would literally run out of offices and restaurants to buy one. Businessmen would call me over and ask what the news was as they dug a nickel out of their pleated suit pants and flipped it to me. There was electricity in the air, and being at the center of it was energizing.

Of the extras I sold, two stick in my mind to this day. First and foremost was the Lindbergh baby kidnapping. It was such a huge event. After years of false heroes—poll sitters and the like—America finally had a true hero again. Then, to have his baby stolen and ultimately killed was simply heartbreaking—for me personally, for our family, and for the nation.

The other extra I remember is when Rice University football star Jack Schulty made All-American. It was not a big story—certainly not the magnitude of the Lindbergh kidnapping—but it stuck in my mind all these years. Maybe it was because Schulty was a real homegrown talent. That story was the first time I truly realized if I worked hard enough, I, too, could do something great.

Our formula for making money was simple but effective. We sold homemade Syrian bread in the morning and papers on the street after school. We called it Syrian bread back then; now it is called pita bread. In the spring, we also sold violets to customers in restaurants and beer joints. In the summer, it was apples for department store customers and employees. We had it down. We were making double our investment, and we just knew that soon we too would be eating at those fancy restaurants.

One night, Johnnie and I were thrown out of Joe's Bar for selling violets. We had been caught many times, but it had never broken our spirits. This time, however, the security guards threatened to call the police. In the end, they didn't catch us, but they did chase us down the street and wave their blackjacks at us. Johnnie and I ran as fast as bullets, taking turns leading, squeezing our money tight in our hands, and yelling over our shoulders to each other, "Hurry, brother! Hurry!" We never left each other behind.

We had a long trek from downtown Houston to our home. Our

route was always north on Houston Street, then through a long, narrow tunnel that let out not far from our house on Freeman Street. The night we got kicked out of Joe's Bar, Johnnie and I ran the entire way to the mouth of the tunnel before stopping to catch our breath.

I can still see the fright on Johnnie's face, half lit by the yellow-orange light of the streetlamps. He was gasping for air and looking around to see if the security guards were after us. We had run more than three miles but were still not thoroughly convinced we were free of them.

Even in the daylight, the tunnel was intimidating—a long corridor of cement that we traversed at least twice a day. It was always dim and damp. It smelled of urine. The bums often found refuge from the elements inside.

That night, my brother and I peered into the inky darkness. The lone lightbulb that illuminated a portion of the tunnel was burned out. For some reason, I suspected a trap. Were the bums planning to steal our night's earnings? Perhaps the security guards had gotten ahead of us and were waiting silently in the blackness. Imaginations can run wild sometimes. I was about to admonish myself for having such thoughts when Johnnie asked the same questions aloud. Maybe I wasn't crazy after all.

In the end, my brother and I mustered our courage, took deep breaths, and entered the abyss. It was slow going at first. We could not see a thing and hugged close to the filthy wall. I swear I would have jumped right out of my skin had we stumbled across anything or anyone. We held our noses; the smell was horrific. When we got to the point where we could see light, we could not contain ourselves and began to run at light speed. Freedom!

We flew up the street, around the corner, and into our house like gangbusters—sweaty, out of breath, and still screaming. I ran into my mother's arms. She was already running toward me. We were finally safe. The fear in her eyes was intense. She hugged me so tight I couldn't breathe.

"What happened? Are you okay? Are you hurt? Talk to me."

The questions came firing out so fast I couldn't answer her. Finally, I caught my breath.

"I am fine, Mom. I am fine!"

"Are you sure, Ralph?"

She turned to Johnnie.

"Are you okay, Johnnie? What happened?"

"Great night, Mom—six cents!" we exclaimed simultaneously.

I didn't want to tell her what really happened because she already worried so much, especially about the two of us. She didn't like the position we had all been forced into, but she was helpless to prevent it.

I handed the pennies to my mother with a smile. She grinned with the kind of love in her eyes that melted me where I stood. As she counted the pennies, however, her face turned grim.

"What's wrong, Mom?" I asked.

"There are only five pennies here, Ralph. Are you sure you had six?"

"Yes, I am sure. I counted them!"

The atmosphere in the room suddenly changed from joy to tragedy, for a penny made a real difference in our existence, in how much food we could buy. Six cents would buy a pint of milk. We needed that penny.

My father walked into the room and stared at me with those

black eyes of his. They bore into me, and I prayed he hadn't heard about the lost penny. My prayers were not answered.

    I tried to shield my brother from my father's wrath, but it seemed like I was failing at everything that day. I often tell people I don't really remember what happened after he walked in, but the truth is that I do. I just don't want to. And I'm not going to describe it here—that would not change what happened anyway. Nothing will. Suffice it to say I took the brunt of it, but Johnnie got a share of it too even though he had done nothing wrong.

    Despite my father, I couldn't help but think about what had happened to that lone penny. When the furious roars and bellowing accusations were over, my little brother and I set out from the kitchen door to make things right. My entire family followed.

    Our only tool was a handful of matchbooks Johnnie and I acquired from some of the hotels and restaurants on our beat. I vaguely remembered having sweaty palms as I had rounded our street corner on the way home, so that's where we started. We must have looked like a swarm of fireflies if someone was witnessing this bizarre event. Six people lighting matches and searching the sidewalk, grass, and street . . . for what? A single penny.

    I felt like we were out there forever. We had gone through almost every match we had. We were all losing hope, searching in the grass for a needle in a haystack, praying to find this lone penny. Then, in the flash as I lit my last match, I saw a flicker in the grass. It seemed like the unmistakable reflection of light off of metal, but I couldn't be positive. I was afraid all the fright and stress of the night was causing me to imagine things. I waved the flame over the grass and saw the glint again. My heart raced.

Ralph at age six, and his brothers Johnnie, George, and Jack, posing for a traveling photographer (whose shadow is visible at the bottom of the photo). This is about the age that Ralph began selling apples and newspapers to help his family survive.

Could it be? I prayed it was. When I reached down, there in the grass was the lone penny.

"I found it! I found it!" I yelled triumphantly.

Everyone came running. We all hugged and cried with joy and happiness.

Today it is almost impossible for me to believe it was only a penny.

WE ONLY KNEW
HOW TO SING

My family depended on my brother Johnnie and me for survival, but our mother was our rock. She kept us grounded, she kept our noses clean, and she kept our clothes spotless. Our mother was the foundation and soul of our family. We adored her and would do anything for her. Her life was hard; she had six children by the time she was twenty-five.

She didn't have a job that brought in a paycheck, but that didn't mean she didn't work. Her delicate hands prepared the mouthwatering foods and beautiful crafts we sold on the street each day.

In our ethnic family, as in so many ethnic families of the time, the women were the backbone and the strength. My mother raised all of us children nearly on her own. And even though she had so much to do each day in our struggle to survive, she always had time for each of us as individuals. Somehow, she knew what each of us needed and was able to give it to us at exactly the right time. For me, it was the tender touch of her hand on the back of my head as I ate her home-cooked bread in the morning. It was her gentle voice telling me about right and wrong, respect, and God as she straightened my clothes before church.

She always reminded us that even though we were poor, we were always to be clean and well dressed. I know now these were the lessons that sustained me throughout my life. I can still feel her compassion and kind spirit. She did everything she could to create something good out of a desperate situation, and her something good was her devotion to raising her children. She talked to us as she cooked, as she cleaned, and as she washed our clothes. If she was ever sad, she never let us see it. I think she could have endured almost anything as long as she knew we kids were all right.

The Lebanese are a close and concentrated community—this was especially true back then—but there are still things we don't talk about, and being severely poor is one of them. We have a great deal of pride.

Christmastime was the hardest for my family, as we were the only people on the block who could not afford to have a tree or gifts. We still don't know who is responsible, but one year one of our neighbors must have told Goodfellows about our plight. Goodfellows is a charity group similar to the Salvation Army, and they help families in need. Two days before Christmas, there was a knock on our door. Standing on the porch were three nurses dressed in blue uniforms with white cuffs and white hats. Two doctors stood next to them, and one was holding a tree—a Christmas tree.

"May I help you?" my mother asked the nurses from the doorway.

"No, we came to help you," the taller nurse replied.

"Help *me*?" Mom questioned. By this time we were all huddled around our mother and peering out in wonder at the five strangers and the Christmas tree.

"Yes," the taller nurse said. "We brought you and your family a Christmas tree with all the trimmings."

There was a moment of silence, and everyone looked at each other in total disbelief. Then the house erupted with cheers and laughter. My mother threw open the screen door, grabbed the nurse's hand, and led her into our tiny home. The others followed. We all danced around them in happiness. We could not contain our excitement. Mom offered refreshments. When they politely declined, I saw relief fall over her face. She didn't have much in the kitchen, but she had to offer, nonetheless.

When they set up the tree, we all sat and watched in amazement. I think we all wanted to help, but the truth of it is we didn't know how. We'd never decorated a Christmas tree before. The nurses hung the ornaments on the branches of the pine tree as the two doctors discussed how they would affix the star to the top. It was like watching a present being unwrapped. With each addition we saw this unimaginable gift come to life. It was unbelievable. Children were supposed to dream of sugarplums. We dreamed of food on the table and full bellies. A Christmas tree was beyond our comprehension.

As they finished, and before they left our humble home, they stood side by side next to the tree and asked us to join them in singing carols. This we knew how to do. I can still hear them singing "Silent Night" and feeling like I was going to cry, partly out of joy for me, my sister, and my brothers, and partly out of happiness for my dear mother. This was our first real Christmas.

As wonderful as our Christmas had been so far, it got even

better on Christmas morning. We all woke up early and found, to our amazement, that Santa Claus had visited our home. Standing shoulder to shoulder, we beamed with exuberance as we beheld the lone red wagon nestled under the tree. The wagon sparkled as the lights from the tree reflected off the shiny candy apple–red paint. We had a real Christmas tree *and* a gift for the first time.

It didn't matter that it was only one gift; what mattered was it was there for us all. I think this is why we are so close even today. We unselfishly shared so much. We learned the true meaning of family, giving, and sacrifice. We always had each other's backs, for we were all we had.

The surprise and joy on my brothers' and sister's faces are still indelibly etched in my memory, as is my mother's quiet, humble grin. I thought then, as I do now, that she was more thrilled than any of us. She was thrilled her children had a present, a tree, and food to eat that night, that she had not let us down. Being poor is not a sin and truly nothing to be ashamed of—except when you're a mother on Christmas morning. At those times, a parent must learn to swallow their pride, choke back the tears, and accept the generosity of others with grace and dignity. And this is just what my mother did that day. Even now, it makes my heart full when I think about it.

We all swelled with a sense of pride as we bolted out the door to the yard with our red wagon in tow. At last, we had something to show off on Christmas Day. We had a wagon to contribute to the group of kids playing on our block. I made sure my younger brothers Louis, George, and Jack were the ones to organize games with our new prize. Our friend Jimmy got the first ride to the end of the street since he always shared his toys with us. Now it was our turn.

The line for rides formed quickly, and each of our friends got one. It didn't matter that it was freezing outside that year, which was not normal for Houston even in December. However, we stayed warm by pulling the wagon and giving rides to everyone on the block.

I saw my mother peeking out the bay window in our front room and smiling. Her eyes were glassy, like she had been crying. I could feel the power of her love toward us kids and her gratitude toward the nurses and doctors of Goodfellows. Their compassion and spirit of giving were the greatest gifts we received. It's what made this the best Christmas ever for our family.

OUR SAVING GRACE

When I think of my mother, I think of sweetness, of flowers blooming, of beautiful music. Our family loved to sing, and we all had good voices ranging from soprano to bass. My mother was the soprano; Louis, Johnnie, and I were tenors; George and Jack sang bass; and Juliette, my beautiful sister, was our only alto. My mother's brother, Albert, conducted our little family symphony. Barrel-chested and jolly, Uncle Albert played the ukulele and sang a raspy chorus while he puffed on his ever-present stogie. Uncle William joined us too, as did Uncle George and Aunt Lula. They were all from my mother's side.

We sang as our after-dinner entertainment. We had no television. Sunday afternoons were special; we sang even more then. We would gather on the porch and serenade passersby. "You Are My Sunshine" was my favorite; "Beautiful Dreamer" was Mother's favorite. At one point we talked of singing professionally as a family, but we focused our efforts on the church instead. Just our family filled out the entire choir.

Orthodoxy was how we were raised; everyone in our Lebanese community belonged to the Antiochian Eastern Orthodox faith.

Ralph at age 3 with his sister Juliette, age 4, in Houston, Texas. Here's an example of how the "portrait studio" has changed—a traveling photographer would bring props (including a live goat) and his camera to neighborhoods so parents could have fun family photos taken.

Ralph about four years old looking dapper in front of the family's humble home in Houston, Texas.

The three pillars of my life, then, now, and always are God, family, and country. I know it sounds simple, perhaps even trite, but these tenets have guided my life for the past eighty-nine years.

When I was a young child, we worshiped in our homes. There were no brick-and-mortar Orthodox churches in Houston. Our priests would travel from city to city and home to home to celebrate the liturgical service. The priest would contact one of the leaders in the community and a service would be arranged. We all knew when church was coming to town. It was the talk of the community. Our traveling priests would give us Communion, baptize our children, marry our young, and bury our dead. I still feel this is the heart and soul of religion. Faith is neither born nor grown in any cathedral. Orthodox Christianity finds its beginning in the book of Acts. For us, our faith is part of our lives. We live and breathe it every day, not just on Sundays.

Orthodoxy and its traditions taught us the power of ritual. Through our religion we learned there is a pace to life. My mother understood this very well and applied it to our everyday lives. I saw it in the way she cooked, kept the house, and even in the way she bathed us.

My sister was always the first in the tub. She was the only girl and thus was given preference. After Juliette was finished, my mother lined us boys up and placed a wooden bench in the middle of our old clawfoot tub. We watched like prisoners waiting to be boiled by cannibals as our mother hauled water from the kitchen. When the tub was full, we stepped in gingerly and arranged ourselves on the squat wooden bench my father made especially for these events. Our backsides were pressed against one another as we waited for our scrubbing.

Mom knelt beside the tub and took a stiff-bristled brush to our skin, especially our ears. She scrubbed so hard our flesh turned pink. We screamed and squealed in pain, but that didn't stop her. She scrubbed until she felt we were clean. We may have been dirt-poor, but we were clean. We bathed every other day. Our clothes were pristine and pressed to perfection.

Our tiny two-bedroom house was spotless as well. We scrubbed the floors—even the porch—with Mom every Wednesday and Saturday. We didn't realize it at the time, but keeping the house so clean would save us a great deal of heartache one day.

At one point, times became so hard that despite our best efforts we could not pay the rent. We just couldn't make ends meet. Mom prepared us for the unthinkable: soon we would be evicted from our home. Our choices were few. We could move in with our grandmother, but if that didn't pan out, we'd be forced to live in a shelter. I could see how much this weighed on dear Mother. She was still young, but the stress of life was turning her old before her time.

My mother had been expecting our landlord to come by for some time, and one fateful Sunday he did. I remember seeing him stand on the street in front of our house. He looked pained. I figured this was going to be nearly as difficult for him as it was for us.

It wasn't long before Mother spied him through the window. I can't imagine what must have gone through her mind, but even now, I am impressed with what she did next. Instead of making Mr. Sanders step up on our porch and knock on the door, dear, sweet, timid Libbie mustered her courage and went out to meet him. I don't know if she meant to or not, but the front door was left ajar. We kids gathered behind it to learn our fate.

As Mother approached the tall, thin man, he removed his hat and even bowed slightly. My mother stood as tall as her five-foot-three frame allowed and held out her hand in greeting. He shook it, and then they both took a half-step backward. Mr. Sanders addressed my mother in a firm yet respectful tone.

"Libbie, it's about the rent."

I saw my mother start to shake ever so slightly. Was this the moment her worst fears would come true? She still stood straight as she crafted her response.

"Mr. Sanders, I have been expecting you. You know I can't pay the rent. I assume you are here to ask us to leave?"

There was a moment of silence between them.

"Libbie, I have given this a great deal of thought, and I want you and your family to stay," he said.

I could see the confusion on my mother's face.

"Why would you do that, sir? You know I can't pay," she said.

"It may be the smallest house on the block, but it is definitely the cleanest. I would rather you and your family continue to stay here than have the house empty or lease it to someone who doesn't take care of it the way you do."

Mom stood motionless, stunned in disbelief. I saw her start to step forward and then stop. I knew she wanted to hug the kind Mr. Sanders, but this was 1935 and she was a married woman. In the end, she did as her instincts insisted and wrapped her arms around Mr. Sanders. It was a sight to behold: my tiny mother squeezing this rail of a man so tightly he could hardly breathe. Mr. Sanders stood there, his arms pinned at his sides, looking down at my mother with a combination of appreciation and embarrassment.

"God will bless you, Mr. Sanders. You are a good man—our

saving grace. When I get the money, I will pay you back every penny," she exclaimed.

"Don't worry about the past, Libbie. I see your struggle. When you can start paying the rent again, just start," he told her.

She thanked him again and again.

Now, as then, I think of my mother as one of the strongest people I have ever known. She may have been diminutive and quiet, but she was like a willow—she bent in a storm but never broke. Her strength was the reason we all survived.

The community knew our situation. Mother was alone most of the time raising six children. She also had to rely on us to help pay the bills. We never minded, for she worked so hard and never complained. Early each morning, I would hear my mother start her daily cooking regimen. She moved with confidence and grace. She had been cooking since she was a small child, and by the time she had us, she had truly honed her skills. My mother was a perfectionist. She told us if it was worth cooking, it was worth doing right. And everything she cooked was perfect in taste, texture, and presentation.

Each night after dinner, our mother would begin the process of bread making. She lined the kitchen table with bedsheets and placed the balls of dough between the sheets so they would rise. She would get up at 2 a.m., knead the bread, make round, frisbee-sized loaves, and let them rise again. She was back up to bake them at 7 a.m. The smell of the divine bread would wake our empty stomachs and cover us like a warm blanket, soothing our souls. To this day, the odor of bread baking brings back memories of my mother and makes me feel like a child, safe in the warm embrace of my family.

As we assembled in the kitchen each morning, Mother would take a single loaf of bread and divide it among us for our breakfast. Then, she lined up baskets on the kitchen table and placed six piping-hot loaves in each one. Our Syrian bread, round and thick, was different, oh-so-different from the loaves of white bread sold in the local bakeries.

Each of us, including Louis, George, and Jack, would grab a basket and go door-to-door selling the bread to our neighbors before school. Every morning, the families in our community waited for our knock at their back doors. They loved my mother's bread. They also loved my mother, which is one of the reasons they bought from us instead of the bakery. Our bread was the envy of the community; it melted in your mouth. They also knew their money was helping support a friend in need.

However, despite our selling out each morning, not everyone loved my mother's bread. Mr. Maxey, the elementary school superintendent, confronted Louis on the street one morning.

"What do you have there, Louis?" he asked curtly.

Embarrassed, Louis stuttered as he told Mr. Maxey it was Syrian bread.

"My mother made it. W-w-w-would you like to buy a loaf?"

Mr. Maxey replied with a stern stare. It was clear our own school superintendent did not approve of our bread, our heritage, or a six-year-old selling goods on the street. Right or wrong, this was the way things worked in those days—in the community, at school, and in business. We knew we were different, but we also knew it was our job to fit in and to become Americans. Looking back, we did all this and more. And while we worked to become integrated into this society, we retained and, in many ways, enhanced our own culture.

It may not have been right for us to feel embarrassed about selling Syrian bread, but it certainly wasn't wrong for us to want to be Americans. Adjusting—giving and taking—is part of being American. I think people today have forgotten this. Our family came here because they wanted what this country has to offer. They wanted the American Dream: to succeed, to be happy, and, above all, to be free.

My parents endured a boat ride across the waters of the Atlantic to come to a country that offered them a better way of life. So, why would we want anything else? We took the good and the bad, embraced it, and became it. We never felt sad or entitled, for we knew this great country gave our family the opportunity for life.

Adaptation is the hallmark of the American identity. That simple fact has enriched me and never diminished me. And no matter how much I love, appreciate, and embrace my heritage, I love being an American more.

A FAMILIAR VOICE

I am feeling uneasy. Something is wrong. My heart races at 110 beats per minute, then plummets into the thirties. I struggle to maintain consciousness. No matter how my heart rate fluctuates, I can hear the voices of my family in the emergency room. The staff at the hospital are constantly reminding us of their policy: Only two visitors at a time. Two people? Are they kidding? We have twenty and it's only a quarter of our family. More are on their way, and there will be no way to keep them out.

With nurses, X-rays, blood work, family in and out, and all the hustle and bustle, my head is spinning. I know the doctors are getting a bit annoyed, but I can't control my family like I used to. I am tired, very tired. I can feel myself slipping in and out of consciousness, and I am unable to distinguish the present from the past. I try to tell the family what I'm thinking, what I want. I can hear them talking over me as if I'm not there. I try to yell, "I am here! Listen to me!" No one hears me. How can this be? I used to be the one they all turned to, but now they are turning without me.

I can't help but think about the years past, about all my family and friends. Is this how it happens? Is this what people think about just before they go? I don't even want to consider this, but at the same time I can't keep the images of friends and family out of my head. I close my eyes and Johnnie is there, real as life, which, of course, is impossible. He's been gone for four years now. I see my life in law school and the face of my beautiful wife, Adelene. I watch the years pass by—the time we spent together, the birth of precious Sharon and my other children, each of them carving out a place in my heart.

Then, without effort, I see my business partners. We are at dinner celebrating a big deal we just closed. Law was my start and is my legacy, but real estate is where I made connections in the city and a sizable property portfolio.

It isn't long before my mind takes me to our church, St. George Orthodox Christian Church, which my family helped build. I walk in the door and see everyone standing in the pews listening to the beautiful music.

Now I'm really worried. I fear it is happening. I've heard people near the end page through their lives.

A familiar voice makes me open my eyes and brings me back to the present. This voice touches the depths of my soul. I look toward the doorway, and in walks my sister, Juliette. All five-foot-two of her is hunched over from osteoporosis, but she is still on her own power. My children greet her with the respect she deserves.

I hear her scold me.

"Ralph, what are you doing now? You need to slow down. When are you going to slow down and stop taking care of everyone else?"

I look into my sister's eyes and smile. I tell her I am okay, but she knows when I am shielding her from the truth, when I'm trying to protect her and the family. This time, when I look at my sweet sister's face and deep into her eyes, I don't see a ninety-one-year-old woman anymore; I see the face and eyes of a nine-year-old girl giving me instructions—my duties for the day. Many times, young Juliette was our mother, our older sister, our disciplinarian, and our confidante. She was the one who kept our family together when my mother was sick or had to be away.

Juliette was my touchstone then, and she still is now. I look into her eyes again and remember when she was in the hospital, not me. That was a long time ago.

JULIETTE

The sign in the window was red and yellow so all could see. Our house was quarantined—a word I didn't understand at first. The doctor and my mother were standing on our porch when Johnnie, Louis, and I returned from school. We were told we could not go inside. Our big, dark eyes must have bulged out of our heads in surprise and dismay.
"What's going on?" we yelled.

Johnnie, Louis, and I all looked at each other trying to figure out the situation. Were we finally being evicted?

"They're kicking us out!" Louis exclaimed.

"Sanders went back on his promise," Johnnie mumbled in disgust.

"I don't believe that," I responded.

I'd seen and heard what he said out on the street to my mother, and I'd believed him. There was something else going on. I looked at my mother, standing on the porch with tears welling up in her eyes. Then, in a soft and apologetic voice, Mother told us what was happening.

"Boys, Juliette has typhoid fever. The house has to be evacuated, disinfected, and sealed. It is a very contagious disease."

Johnnie, Louis, and I all looked at each other again, wondering what would happen next. Where would Juliette go? Where would we go? And how did this happen?

We were clean. Our clothes were clean. Our house was clean. Our mother made sure of that. How could our lovely Juliette contract such a terrible disease? This was scary for poor Juliette and for our whole family. Would she survive?

Mother explained Juliette would have to be isolated in the hospital. The good news was that none of the rest of us had any symptoms. The doctor thought Juliette might have contracted the disease from her nine-year-old friend Michael, who lived down the street. She had gone to visit him the day before they quarantined his house. Now Juliette was sick with a high fever.

My mother was trying to figure out our next steps. Juliette would go to the hospital, but where would the rest of us go? I know deep down that my mother was horrifically embarrassed. How would she explain this to her husband and the rest of the community? What about her flowers and Syrian bread? Who would eat food from a typhoid house?

Juliette had stayed home from school that day; she had been unable to get out of bed. My mother had called the doctor, who came immediately (doctors made house calls back then). He examined Juliette in the room the four of us shared. Mother later told us about how nervous and shy Juliette was when the doctor asked to see her abdomen. Timidly she had raised her gown, and on her stomach were three rosy spots. The doctor pressed them and asked if they hurt.

"Yes!" she'd cried.

Dr. Dunham told my mother, "Juliette has to be moved to the hospital and the house has to be quarantined."

Mother was panicked.

"What do I do with the boys?" she asked.

"They will have to find somewhere else to stay," Dr. Dunham replied.

My mother's strength drained out of her body and puddled at her feet. She could not argue, for he was the doctor, and she knew her little girl was very sick. As we stood on the porch with Mother and the doctor, the orderlies came for Juliette and took her to Hermann Hospital. We all had to find other places to stay, which was not easy because everyone knew we had been exposed to typhoid. In times like these, family is so important. My grandmother, Annie Faour, took all of us in. I don't know what we would have done without her.

Juliette was in the hospital for just over three months. We were lucky the health department quarantined our house for only a month, but our time away was so much easier than Juliette's. We had each other, while she was all alone. We visited the hospital but were never allowed to enter her room. We weren't even permitted on her floor.

Mother arranged with the hospital for us to see Juliette every Saturday, so we developed a new routine. Every Saturday morning, we piled into the Model T Ford we'd somehow acquired and trekked to Hermann Hospital. It sounds impossible now, but it took us an hour to drive ten miles from North Main to the medical center.

We must have looked like something out of *The Grapes of*

Wrath—Dad behind the wheel, Mom next to him, and us five boys stuffed wherever there was room. We took turns sitting by the windows so we could hang our heads out the side of the car and feel the wind on our faces. It was quite a thrill. The dirt roads of Houston were well traveled and full of ruts. I was always afraid one of those bicycle-thin tires on the Model T would burst and we'd be left to walk. Thankfully, they didn't—well not on this trip, anyway.

Once we arrived at the hospital, Mother lined us up for inspection, from tallest to shortest. If we were lucky, she would just brush the dust from our clothes. If we weren't, she would moisten her handkerchief and give us a spit bath the way only a mother can. Afterward, we stood below Juliette's window and waited for the appointed time to see her.

"Stand tall!" Mother would say. "Smile for Juliette."

Standing shoulder to shoulder, we looked up to the fourth-story window in anticipation of her arrival. The nurses, God bless them, would wheel our sister in her hospital bed over to the window; she would lean forward and crane her neck to see us. When she appeared in the window, we would jump up and down, yelling up to her to get well soon. We missed her so much.

At one point, my father became so distraught that he actually sneaked in the back door and ran four flights up the stairwell to her room. He was so anxious to see her. When Juliette saw him at her door, her eyes filled with tears of joy. She was so lonely with no family or friends to talk to, play with, or tell her she was going to be all right.

The nurse caught my father.

"What are you doing here, sir? You must leave this room immediately!" she yelled.

"But I am her father!" I think he must have yelled back.

"I don't care who you are. You must leave now. This is a restricted area," she replied sternly.

The yelling match continued, with my father insisting he could stay because he had typhoid fever as a child. Seeing the pain on his face, the nurse embraced him and sadly said, "I am so sorry, sir, but you have to leave."

The nurse was in the right, but I'll never forget the look in my father's eyes as he was escorted out of the hospital. No father ever wants to fail his children, and I'm sure he felt like he had failed little Juliette that day. Typhoid fever, along with many other diseases, is no longer a threat to our society largely due to the efforts of our medical professionals and strong, well-crafted, and disciplined public health policy. This may be an enduring benefit of our society, but it was little consolation to an anguished father and a heartbroken nine-year-old.

While in the hospital, Juliette was given two blood transfusions and a multitude of medications. In the 1930s, scientists had not yet discovered antibiotics. The transfusions—one from Aunt Lula and the other from Uncle George—helped, as did the medications. Juliette recovered, but the disease had a serious impact on her. She lost her hair, and her left leg ended up shorter than her right. While she was in the hospital, the nurses placed weights on her left foot in an effort to lengthen her leg. Every day, the weights pulled on Juliette's leg with the goal of stretching it back to normal so she would be able to walk again. Her spirit was strong. She was an amazing girl who persevered through challenges that would have sent a grown man to his knees.

After three months of hospitalization, Juliette was released.

The nurses wheeled her out to the cheers of her exuberant family. We were all so happy to have her back with us, but we were also worried. Would Juliette be able to walk?

I wish I could tell you when Juliette got home everything was clear sailing, but I can't. It wouldn't be the truth. I'm afraid that the world is not always a fair and compassionate place. After returning home from her stint in the hospital, Juliette was weak. Those months lying in bed had atrophied her muscles. At first, she was confined to her bed. Then she was in a wheelchair, as she was unable to walk. Each day, the nurses came by the house for therapy.

Juliette's convalescence was long and arduous. The weights at the hospital did not work as planned, so young Juliette had to learn how to walk again, step by trembling step. At first, it was a struggle for her simply to cross the room, but she would not be deterred. This was just another obstacle in life, and if our family had learned anything, it was how to overcome, adapt, and improvise. We were taught to meet life head-on. If life threw you a curveball, you learned to hit curveballs. Pouting and complaining were not allowed and not even considered, really—there was no time for them. We all learned to take care of ourselves and each other.

Juliette began walking again by traversing from chair to chair across our small living room like a toddler. After only a few weeks, she graduated, step by step, to walking without assistance. Mother was with her every minute of the day and encouraged her at every turn.

By the time Easter rolled around, young Juliette was finally able to go outside. We boys were vaulting over the six stairs of the porch onto the grass below, which was a favorite game of ours. We heard the front door open, and to our surprise, Juliette emerged. We stood in awe as she stepped out of the shadows, lifted her face, and soaked in the rays of the warm sun. We all watched for a moment and then, unable to help ourselves, we surrounded her and cheered. We jumped with excitement, for we were together. Our oldest sister, caretaker, and best friend was with us again.

All of a sudden, Juliette broke loose from our circle and began to run for the stairs. She took a giant leap off the porch, landed on the grass, and rolled. We were all in shock. Our jaws hit the ground. We held our breath for fear she had hurt herself. But when she rose to her feet and gave us that sweet, mischievous smile, we knew she was okay. She was back! She was finally back! I think someone could have knocked us over with a feather.

Juliette missed most of the school year, and at some point, it was decided she would simply skip the year and start over again in the fall. This put my older sister and me in the same grade and fostered a situation I would regret for the rest of my life.

Juliette and I walked to school together every day. It was as natural as anything we did. The first fall we were in the same grade, Juliette wore a bonnet on her head. Her hair had still not fully grown back. After she came home from the hospital it fell out by the handful, much to the anguish of Mother, who often stared at Juliette with the saddest of looks on her face. After a while, Mom simply shaved Juliette's hair off with a pair of clippers. Believe it or not, it was an improvement over the tufts of hair dotting her scalp. Besides, the doctor said a full shave might stimulate growth.

At school, Juliette was greeted by all the teasing and cruel jokes expected from a group of young boys. Ours was a selfish age when peers ridiculed anything and anyone who was different in any way. The boys at school could not resist making fun of Juliette. They ran up behind her, stuck their fingers through the hole in her bonnet, and said mean things about her baldness. They always brought Juliette to tears. It brings me no joy to admit I, too, was part of the teasing.

One day in a class where Juliette sat in front of me, I did the meanest thing I can ever remember—and to my sister no less. In a flash of mischievousness and cruelty, I pulled her bonnet off when the teacher was out of the room. I knew the other kids would laugh and jeer, and I was right. It happened just as I planned. What I didn't plan on was the hurt in Juliette's eyes when she looked over her shoulder and realized I was her tormentor. The disbelief and betrayal on her face shattered my heart. I have never felt so despicable in my life. It was, without a doubt, the worst trick I ever played on anyone.

The realization of what I had done to my loving sister who had helped shepherd our small band for so long brought me to my knees. I apologized profusely. Juliette forgave me and never mentioned it again. However, I don't know if I have ever been able to forgive myself.

Ultimately, Mrs. Crawford, the school principal, sent out an edict to all students and parents: Anyone caught teasing or harassing Juliette would be expelled from school on the spot. With that, the teasing stopped, and Juliette was finally able to attend school with grace and dignity—a relief to her and to all of us.

HE WAS NOT GOING TO MAKE IT ON HIS OWN

We loved playing games, especially baseball. When my brothers and I gathered in our front yard the boys down the street would often call us over for a game. My four brothers and I gave our team an advantage: We were the infield, and we were good.

It was a wonderful day. Fall in the South is like summer anywhere else. The sky was a crisp blue, so bright we had to squint just to look at it. Our "field" was the Jamails' yard, the largest in the neighborhood. It had natural bases: the porch was first, a fence post second, and a giant oak was third. Home plate was the center of the driveway. The Jamails kept the grass green, and they had just mowed that morning. To top it off, we had a nearly new baseball—a far cry from the dirty, scuffed balls we were used to playing with. We couldn't believe how lucky we were. I think we all secretly pretended we were Major League players competing for a pennant that day. After all, that's what teenage boys do.

The bases were loaded, and my brother Johnnie was on the

mound. At home plate stood Tony Covezzi, who didn't like Johnnie because he was jealous of him. Johnnie got all the girls. His personality won them over every time—not to mention the single black curl that fell perfectly on the center of his forehead. Girls just couldn't resist him.

Before his windup, Johnnie looked Tony square in the eyes as if to say, *I'm gonna strike you out.*

Tony stood tall. His body seemed to respond, *Oh yeah? Get ready—this is gonna be a home run.*

Tony leaned into the pitch, the bat connected to the ball . . . and *smack*! It was a line drive headed straight for Johnnie. An instant later my brother was face down on the ground. No one moved for a moment. Then I ran over to him and turned him over. Blood was everywhere. Tony's line drive had hit Johnnie straight in the face. His nose was completely smashed. The blood was tremendous. Instinctively, I picked him up, threw him on my back, and headed to Jefferson Davis Hospital. I ran until I couldn't run anymore. It was a long way, and Johnnie was bleeding badly.

"Johnnie, can you walk? I don't think I can take another step!" I said, looking over my shoulder, out of breath.

He slipped off my back onto his feet and tested his balance.

"Sure, brother," he said hesitantly.

We slowly walked a block or two. Looking at his blood-soaked shirt, I realized he was not going to make it on his own and we needed to get to the hospital immediately. I grabbed his shoulders and heaved him onto my back once more, running the rest of the way to the hospital. I don't know how far it was; I only know that when I got to the door of the emergency room I nearly collapsed. I propped Johnnie up in a chair and I tried to find a doctor.

"I need help! I need help!" I yelled.

No one was around. I saw a door behind the nurses' station and ran to open it. There sat two doctors and a nurse eating their lunch.

"Fix my brother! Hurry, he's hurt!" I yelled.

They jumped out of their chairs, ran over to Johnnie, and picked him up. They asked me if I needed help.

"No, please, just help my brother!" I gasped.

The nurse asked how I got there. When I told her the story, she was a bit shocked and amazed that I had carried my brother so far.

After a few moments, I found Johnnie being tended to in the ER. A nurse and a doctor were looking over him. For a brief moment, I feared for his life. Then the nurse spied me in the doorway and winked. It was a simple gesture, but it was all I needed to know that Johnnie would be all right. I felt the weight of the world lifted from my shoulders.

I smiled at the nurse and found my way to the waiting room. I needed to sit down. The chair was stiff and cold; the room was empty. I took inventory of myself for the first time since the incident. I remember feeling two things. One, the pain in my lower back. Two, my heart was racing faster than I'd ever felt it before.

I was overwhelmed at the thought of losing my brother, my best friend. I looked up, and the doctor walked out of the ER toward me.

"Are you the one who carried the baseball player in?"

"Yes, sir. That's my brother, Johnnie. Is he going to be okay?" I asked with anticipation.

The doctor was matter-of-fact in his response.

"Your brother will be just fine."

I was so relieved to hear the good news that I wanted to hug him.

"We will have to reset his badly broken nose. He will be ready to go home in a few hours, and back on the mound in no time," the doctor said with a reassuring smile.

"Thank you so much for taking such good care of my brother, Doctor. How much do I owe you?"

The doctor paused for a moment and inspected me from head to toe, then with a slight grin, he said, "You don't owe us anything. We are running a special for baseball players this week."

Now, I really wanted to hug him. I knew he was making up a story, but I was happy to go along with it. I shook his hand firmly, thanked him before he departed, and then sat down to wait for my brother.

I GIVE YOU HELL

Soon after Johnnie recovered from his smashed nose, my family decided to take a trip in our old Model T Ford. It was the spring of 1938, and we were going to visit my father's mother in Elgin, Texas. We didn't take many trips in those days. Gasoline was expensive at seventeen cents per gallon, and paying for a motel room was out of the question. But we were all excited to see our grandmother again. She always had beds for us—a particular treat for Johnnie and me since we had no bed at home.

Two years earlier, my brother and I had made the trip to Elgin on our own. Dad bought us train tickets and we rode the rails all the way from Houston's Union Station to the small town of Elgin, which is just outside Austin. I was twelve and Johnnie was ten. In those days, the special arrangements for unescorted minors consisted of a short conversation and a handshake between my father and the conductor.

We spent most of the trip with our heads out the window. We were amazed at the sights, sounds, and speed of the train. The Missouri–Kansas–Texas Railroad was like a dream to us, and we gleefully listened as the engineer blew the whistle one time for each car in the train. We had traversed Houston on our own many times, but this was different. This was like one of the adventures Johnnie and I had read about in books. We could have been on the Orient Express or traveling by train across Africa.

It wasn't until we reached Elgin and saw our grandmother, Sadie, that we realized our faces were smudged with soot from the smokestack. It was a coal-burning engine, and in our excitement, we simply hadn't realized our faces and shirts had gotten darker and darker with every passing mile that we kept our heads out the window.

Our grandmother was aghast when she spied us across the small station in Elgin. In truth, I don't think she recognized us at first—our faces were nearly black, and our thick black hair was standing on end from the wind. When she did recognize us, she whisked us off to her house and proceeded to scrub us clean, scolding us just as our own mother would have done.

This time, our family trip to Elgin was by car instead of train, but we were all equally excited. We talked and joked as we piled into the Model T for the 167-mile drive. It took us over seven hours. My brothers and I sat in the back, as usual, Juliette and Mother sat in the passenger seat together, and Father drove. He always drove. I don't think I remember my mother driving even once, but that wasn't unusual for those days.

Spring in Texas can be a wonderful and beautiful time. The prevailing winds are still out of the northwest, holding off the summer humidity. Bluebonnets and Indian paintbrush line the roads, showing off their colors to the passing travelers.

My family and I started out from our home in Houston just after 9 a.m. We planned on leaving earlier, but it was almost impossible to organize our tribe of eight (not much has changed over the years, I fear). We were so excited we could hardly sit still, and this caused my father to issue several edicts, none of which we followed. His voice had a stern tone, but it was nonthreatening somehow. Even my father was not immune to getting a little excited and happy when taking a trip out of town.

We drove at the incredible speed of just over thirty miles per hour—which was fast in those days. And while Houston is mostly flat, there are rolling hills as you get close to Austin and the Balcones Fault Zone. The Model T was a great automobile for its time, but it did have one distinctive flaw: the fuel was gravity-fed to the engine, which meant the car had to be pushed up big hills because the fuel would not flow.

My brothers and I were the horses, so to speak, who pushed our black Model T up the steeper hills on the way to Elgin. Dad did his best to get the car over the hills by gunning the engine on the downhill side, but sometimes we didn't make it over the top of the next one. This was when we boys sprang out of the backseat and pushed like a team of Olympic bobsledders. Mom and Juliette stepped out and walked along the side of the road to lighten the load. Dad stationed himself just outside the driver's side and pushed as he steered. I can still hear him now.

"Push harder! Don't stop!"

We all listened to his commands and did our best to comply.

Once we got to the top of a hill, we all piled back in. For us boys, this was an opportunity to change our seating and rotate someone new to the window. It didn't take long for our family to fall into a rhythm. Mother and Juliette began to sing songs in the front, and after my brothers and I caught our breath, we joined in.

Singing was always a great pastime for us, and it was as rewarding in the car as it was at home with our aunts and uncles. The time passed quickly when we sang.

Mother had prepared peanut butter and jam sandwiches for the trip. It was Friday, so we fasted from meat and dairy. You might think Friday was a difficult day, but to the contrary. Friday was a day when we all ate the same for a reason: our commitment to our faith.

God reveals himself in many ways and at odd times. Our family's commitment to Orthodoxy is strong, but our commitment to each other is even stronger. That day, in the car, it all came together for me: my family and my faith. Seeing my father in the driver's seat, my mother passing out the food and singing, and my brothers and me in the back doing as we were told, I realized life was hard, but we had each other and we had God. He will never forsake us, and my family will never forsake each other. In the good times and the bad we are together, and God is there just the same.

Before we ate, we prayed and made the sign of the cross, for our faith was with us all the time, even in the car. Orthodoxy is full of tradition—the church offers a liturgical service that touches all the senses. There is incense to smell, raising our awareness to heaven. There are icons to see of those who have gone before us in faith. There is beautiful music to hear and Communion—the essence of our church, the body and blood of Christ—to taste. The church offers a way to grow in your faith and reach oneness with God. It is there for anyone if they choose. We choose.

We ended the long trip with squeaky breaks and a cloud of dust. We were finally in the parking lot of Grandmother Sadie's icehouse, the southern name for a beer joint. She had become a legend in our family. We exited our small car to stretch our legs, and she appeared on the porch of her establishment. My father was the first to greet her. She had raised him alone as a single mother, and his heart was with her at all times.

We all jumped onto the porch and greeted her with kisses before we ran into the icehouse for candy and soda, an unusual treat in those days. My grandmother made candy in the back of her icehouse and baked the most incredibly delicious cakes on a wood-burning stove. How anyone could bake on a wood-burning stove was completely beyond me, but she did it with regularity, and each time it was better than the last.

We arrived early in the afternoon and spent our time playing in the aisles of the small grocery store attached to the icehouse. The icehouse was located in the back. Grandmother Sadie had candy stocked in cupboards and bowls, along with Coca-Colas in refrigerated cases for five cents each. Grandmother gave us two, and we shared them. My mother would not allow us to have any more. Then, we each got one piece of candy. That was the best of all, because we didn't have to share, which was a rarity.

Even in the early afternoon she had drinking customers. I think I remember Prohibition being in effect, but this was small-town Texas and that's just the way things worked. Besides, Sadie just served beer, no hard liquor, and there was really no sin in having an icehouse in Texas. Hardworking men always need a place to gather.

Sadie didn't live at her icehouse; she lived four blocks away, which was where we slept at night. However, her home was not where the action happened. My grandmother was five feet tall and equally broad. Sadie's Place served everyone—whites, Blacks, and Mexicans. The men loved her, and she kept an orderly bar.

There was a three-foot-high wall that divided the bar along racial lines: a small section for the Blacks and the Mexicans, and the rest for the whites. Sadie hated the wall and the law that made her put it up. She neither enforced nor believed in the racial divide. The men all worked together picking cotton every day, so it didn't make sense that now, at her icehouse, they had to sit in separate areas because of their skin color. After all, Sadie, figured, her skin color was different from them all. She was Syrian Lebanese.

Sadie was tough and a good businesswoman. The vendors delivered drinks to the bar and goods to the store.

"Miss Sadie," they would say, "give me a minute while I add up what you owe me."

While the salesman sat at the bar tallying up the bill, my grandmother would walk over to the cash register, pull out the money drawer, and walk back to the bar. Before the salesman arrived at a sum, she would hold out the money and in her broken English would say, "Here, this is what I owe you."

She was always right. The salesmen were always astounded.

Sadie was tough with her customers when she had to be. Sometimes the men would get rowdy after a few beers. When the music and men got too loud, out came her stick—a three-inch-thick, two-foot-long oak board that had been broken off of the wall she hated so much. She kept it at the end of the bar just for these occasions. My tiny grandmother would slam the board on the bar and yell.

"Quiet! Do you want them to close me down?"

From the early 1900s. Sadie, Ralph's grandmother, behind the bar at her icehouse in Elgin, Texas. She knew how to keep the regulars in line.

Then, she would walk out from behind the safety of her bar, stand in the middle of the men, and shake the board at them.

"I give you hell. Do you hear me? I give you hell," she'd say.

When Miss Sadie spoke, everyone listened, and the room fell silent. The saloon became calm, the music softer, and the men friendlier.

Sometimes the men would tease my grandmother out of good humor. They would purposefully start a ruckus in the corner of the bar just to get her riled up. Then they would keep it up until they heard the whack of her stick on the bar. When they got her to yell, "I give you hell!" these massive men, who worked in the fields and were callused and harder than oaks, would all bow down and say, "Please, Miss Sadie, don't hurt us! Please!"

I learned early that the stature of a person is not what commands respect, it is their character. My grandmother was always fair; she treated everyone who set foot in her bar the same. You might think her attitude was born from her heritage or from her status as an immigrant, but I don't see it that way. Not at all. Hers may have been the mindset of an immigrant, but it was also the conviction of someone who takes stock of herself and refuses to be taken care of by others.

HIGHWAY 290

Our weekend in Elgin flew by. It was Sunday afternoon before I knew it, and we were piling back into our Model T Ford. My grandmother packed our car with food, candy, and soda. We thought we were in heaven. Back in Houston, Johnnie and I would stand in the middle of the candy store after selling our goods. We could not afford the sweets, so we just breathed in the aroma. Here in Elgin, we not only smelled but also tasted the candy. It was wonderful. Treats like these were so unusual to us. We could feel the excitement.

The seating arrangement in the car was the same on the way home—Dad driving, Mother and Juliette in the passenger seat, and all of us boys in the back. We were all sad to leave Tita's house (*Tita* is Arabic for "grandmother"), but we were excited to take another road trip. Driving, singing, eating, and talking together was a gift for us. *This could not get better*, I remember thinking at the time.

After driving for almost three hours, the sun began to set behind us. We were headed east, and the soft light of dusk surrounded us. My brothers and I were playing some silly game in the back when Mother and Juliette began to unwrap our evening meal. Dad actually seemed happy; I thought I heard him humming along to the tune Juliette and my mother were singing. Suddenly, we heard the engine sputter . . . then cough . . . gasp . . . and stop. At first, I thought we were on a hill and the engine was starved for fuel. But when I looked out, the road was flat.

"Dad, what's wrong?" We all yelled at the same time.

Dad did not reply. He only gripped the wheel and stared at the gauges. The car rolled to a slow, definitive stop. We were broken down on Highway 290, a two-lane dirt road. It was late, dark, and there was no one else on the road. I could see the frustration on my father's face as all of us looked to him for an answer. We got out of the car and pushed it to the side of the road. When my father opened the hood, smoke billowed out. Dad was not mechanical. He knew this was out of his league and he needed to get help. He announced he was going to walk to the nearest town and call a relative to come get us.

We were all a bit shocked.

"What are we to do, Dad?" I asked.

"Son," he said with a pat on my head, "you are to watch over the family until I return."

This was the first time I remember him saying this to me out loud, but it was certainly not the first time I felt the responsibility.

We all watched Dad walk down the road in the dim light. It wasn't long before his hulking figure merged with the darkness. In one way or another, I think I have remembered him in this way for most of my life—walking off into the distance and disappearing as we all looked on.

Night was falling fast and I remember a feeling of fear coming over my body. I didn't want to show it, though, because my father said I needed to take care of Mother and the family. We had been on our own before many times, but this was different. This was not Houston, and it definitely was not the city. In Houston, we knew our surroundings, where to find food and shelter, and how to survive. We had family and friends nearby. Here on the side of the road, we were truly in the wilderness. There were no cars, no houses, not even the glow from the yard light of a distant farm.

We waited for several hours. Still no cars. We talked, sang, and ate the last of the food Tita had packed for us. We never said it aloud, but we all wondered when our dad would be back. How long were we to be on the side of the road? The youngest boys, George and Jack, didn't realize the peril we were in. Instead of sitting frozen in fear, they played. We watched as they jumped on and off the running board of the car and slipped into the back window on one side of the car and out the other. I just sat there and worried. *What were we to do? What if Dad didn't return?*

I looked over at my mother and Juliette, who were sitting on the grass and holding each other. Then, I heard the sound of an engine approaching. I looked up the road and saw nothing for a few moments until I saw a light appear over the horizon. It was coming our way. I stood up.

"It's Dad! It's Dad!" I yelled.

In the very next instant, I realized the car was coming from the wrong direction. I yelled at George and Jack to come over to Mom so all of us could get close together. We stood in a huddle, our eyes bulging. I did not know if I should try to flag the car down or let it go by. The car slowed when its occupants saw us standing there. They pulled over and asked if we needed help. I was about to say yes when Mother spoke up.

"No, thank you. My husband has gone to the next town for help. He should be back any moment," she said.

"Are you sure, ma'am?" the man asked with genuine concern on his face. "This isn't the safest place to be."

"I am sure," she said. "We will wait for my husband."

We watched as the man drove off in the still darkness. There was no moon that night, and I don't think I knew until then just how dark the world could get. I knew my mother was right to turn down the help of a stranger and wait for our dad—loyalty was her hallmark—but we were so alone, afraid, and vulnerable. The night dragged on, and we ended up sleeping in the car. Johnnie and I took turns standing watch, but even when it was my turn to sleep, I couldn't. All I could do was watch, listen, and pray.

Sometimes you find God in a well-lit church, and sometimes you find Him in the pitch dark on the side of the road. When I look back, I know this was a pivotal moment in my spiritual journey. I was grateful my parents had given me a faith that was real, tangible, and gave me strength to pull from when I was sitting in that pitch-black darkness on the side of the road. As I prayed, the fear in my body seemed to wane, and calm came over me. I knew even out here, we were in God's hands and we would be all right.

As the sun began to rise, I heard a car engine. This time it was coming from the right direction. I got up slowly because I didn't want to wake anyone or get them excited unnecessarily. The car pulled over, stopped, and out came Dad and Aunt Lula. I was never so glad to see my father. I began to yell.

"Get up! Get up! Dad is here! Dad is here!"

My father gave me a tight hug, not something he did very

often. He stared at me, and in his eyes, I could see gratitude and peace because we were all okay.

We stuffed ourselves into Aunt Lula's car, all nine of us sitting on top of each other.

"What about the car?" I asked Dad.

I couldn't imagine leaving something so valuable.

"Andy is sending a tow truck," he replied.

Andy owned a mechanic shop on North Main, not far from our house.

The ride home was quiet, which was unusual for our family, but the time passed quickly. We arrived at our tiny house on Freeman Street by midmorning. Tired and dirty from our long night, we dragged ourselves inside. We kids feared Mother would pull out the bathtub—and that is exactly what she did.

THIS IS ONLY A TRIAL

By the time I was in junior high school, things had improved marginally for our family. We all had our jobs down; each of us was bringing in money. My mother saved every extra penny she could. In addition to my other jobs, I landed a part-time job at the local grocery store. The lure of a steady paycheck was just too great. So, while my friends were out on dates on Friday and Saturday nights, I spent my time unloading crates of vegetables, sacking groceries, helping ladies to their cars, and hoping for tips.

The grocery was a steady job and paycheck, but I worked the longest for the *Houston Chronicle*. Once a year, they selected a paperboy as most likely to succeed, and in 1932 they chose me. My picture was framed in an ad with bold letters across the top: *Most Likely to Attend College*. I was the celebrity of the neighborhood, and I enjoyed the notoriety this gave my family and me. Life looked a little brighter in 1932. It was also the year my mother got her first modern appliance.

I arrived home from school one afternoon to find the delivery man, Mr. Bradshaw, putting a block of ice in our icebox. Yes, that is how we cooled our perishables back then.

"Hello, Mr. Bradshaw. How are you today?" I greeted him. He was a nice man who always helped my mother.

"I am great, Ralph. How are you?" Mr. Bradshaw replied.

"I am good, sir. How is the ice business these days?"

I always imagined the ice business to be very successful in hot Houston.

"Well, not as good as it used to be," Mr. Bradshaw answered. "Electric refrigerators are taking over."

Electric refrigerators? I thought. *Only the rich and famous can afford those.*

Mr. Bradshaw explained they were now offering secondhand electric refrigerators, and we could try one on approval for a week if we wanted. I looked at my mother and saw her shaking her head slowly, so only I noticed. I knew she was thinking we couldn't afford it. I looked alternately at Mr. Bradshaw and my mother. Then I turned back to Mr. Bradshaw and asked, "Do you have one with you?"

His eyes opened wide with surprise.

"Yes, I do," he said.

"This is only a trial, you understand. We will probably send it back at the end of the week," my mother announced at first.

"How much does this luxury item cost?" I boldly asked Mr. Bradshaw.

"Well, since it is used, it would be forty-nine ninety-five," he said.

"There is no way we can buy it unless we can pay it out over time," she said emphatically.

I don't know if people were more willing to work with you then, or if we just had honest faces, but he agreed to $3 a month until it was paid off. It would take us a year and a half. We sealed the deal with a handshake, not a contract. Back then, your word was your bond, and a person was nothing without their word.

The large, white enamel refrigerator stood proudly where the old, dilapidated icebox used to reside. The contrast was stark. I could see my mother doing her best to contain herself, but she was not doing a very good job of it. She paced back and forth with excitement. She looked at it, and then touched the clean, white surface of the electric appliance. I think she would have slept in the kitchen that night if she could have.

I'd heard what she said, but all I could see was the glimmer in her eyes and the girlish grin on her face. What a convenience this would be for my mother, whose cooking was the envy of the community and a mainstay of our existence.

After Mr. Bradshaw left, my mother pulled me aside. I could see the pain on her face. She was trying to speak but the words would not come. I knew what she was going to ask before she could even say it. She started to ask three times before finally getting the words out.

Looking at the floor she whispered, "Ralph, I know you already do so much to support us, and you have school, too. This will not be possible without you making the extra three dollars a month, which is a lot of money."

She paused and looked at me with her sweet, beautiful face.

"Do you think you can do this, my son?"

"Of course," I said as I hugged her.

I knew this was going to be very difficult for me. But my hardship was nothing compared to hers. If I could give her a little happiness and share her burdens, it was worth it to me.

Ralph, likely at age fifteen. At that age, Ralph attended school while working about three jobs.

I never said a word to Juliette or my brothers about the commitment my mother and I made, but they certainly suspected it. When they saw me working extra hard, they knew the truth. I was so happy to be able to do something so wonderful for her. My siblings did what they could, too. Without fanfare, they each put a small portion of their earnings in my hand every week. It was only pennies, but when pennies are what you have, pennies are all you can give. I knew why they were doing it, so I took the money as the gift it was. They had not made the deal with the salesman and their reputations were not on the line, but they made it their obligation because we are family and we always looked after one another.

With a modern refrigerator in the house, we were all starting to feel good about ourselves. Oh, we still lived in a two-room house in North Houston, but having an electric appliance made us feel like we were doing pretty well—the American Dream was starting to come true for us. Even Dad, who scraped for work after being laid off from the Ford Motor plant in town, was doing better. He, like the rest of us, found a way to survive and even prosper by cobbling together odd jobs. Before the market crash of 1929, Dad refinished and tuned pianos, and with the fall in the economy, instruments like pianos became luxury items. However, this ended up providing my father with an unexpected job.

One day Barclay Piano Company called my father. They had a new job for him: repossessing pianos. It wasn't exactly what he wanted to do, but it was work. Unfortunately, in those days, repossessing items was becoming more common. Families who had prospered before the crash could no longer afford to keep some of their most cherished items.

Dad's first job was to take back a piano from the home of Mr. Schmidt, a longtime, loyal customer of Barclay's. Dad showed up at the front door with a repossession notice in his hand. Mr. Schmidt did not greet him with grace, for his anger was all-consuming. Losing a family's prized possession is more than some people can handle, and his anger was misdirected to the messenger, my father. Mr. Schmidt blocked the door and ordered my father to leave. Dad apologized and said he needed to take the instrument that day. Dad assured Mr. Schmidt if he could give him more time he would, but this was not his decision. My father had a great appreciation for a man's dignity.

The two men stood still and stared at each other for a moment. Dad had his job to do. Mr. Schmidt may have been in a somewhat better financial position than Dad was, but it was clear his world was starting to crumble. Over the man's shoulder, my dad could see there were few pieces of furniture left in the house. The piano was one of the last, along with a small table and a couple of old wooden chairs. After a short while, the two men bowed their heads. Neither wanted to be in this predicament, but they were.

Finally, Mr. Schmidt stood aside and allowed my father to pass.

"Where's your helper?" the man asked Dad.

"I don't have one, Mr. Schmidt," my father said. "I have to do this on my own."

Mr. Schmidt looked at Dad in disbelief. My father was not a tall man at five-foot-nine, but he had the strength of many men, with a chest as big around as a whisky barrel. It didn't matter how big you were, though, moving a piano by yourself was hard, backbreaking work. Mr. Schmidt watched as my father muscled the upright piano from the wall. He realized my father could perform this seemingly insurmountable task, but he also realized how difficult and dangerous it was. My father got behind the huge wooden instrument and began to shove. His face reddened and beads of sweat formed on his forehead. Dad rolled the piano halfway across the floor, then Mr. Schmidt stepped in to help him. No matter how angry he was about losing the piano, he could not stand by and watch another man struggle.

The two men got the piano out to the street and onto the truck in less than an hour. They parted with a handshake and a renewed respect for one other; they realized they were both doing all they could to take care of their families in desperate times.

I AM NOT AN ABORIGINE

Although we boys needed to work to sustain ourselves, Mother and Juliette never let any of us neglect our studies. They knew what generations of immigrants have known for centuries: Education is the road to prosperity. I cannot honestly tell you I was a model student. I worked hard and did my homework almost all the time, but the reality of selling bread in the morning, delivering papers in the afternoon, and working at the local grocery on the weekends left little time for academic pursuits. I don't know if I would have been a straight A student even if I'd had the time. I was a solid B student—it was just the way I was built. I was a quick study, but I was never going to be happy sitting and reading in a library. There was too much to do outside. There was money to be made.

I was shy back in junior high school. I guess a lot of boys are. At that age, I just didn't know what I was made of yet. It took a while to develop my confidence. From my first day at school, I was self-conscious about my heritage. None of the other kids really knew what a Lebanese person was. They only knew we had dark skin, dark hair, and we ate strange food. Though they are chic today, in 1937, hummus and Syrian bread (pita bread) were completely unknown to most people.

Lunch at school was usually an adventure. Mother packed our lunch every day. She used Syrian bread instead of the white bread that the other kids ate. We often kept to ourselves during lunch. We cupped the pita bread in our hands and alternately took quick bites of bread, grape leaves, and kibbeh. No one else had food like this. Sometimes we would even hide in the corner, behind a door, or wherever we could be alone, so no one would laugh at us or ask us questions.

Many days we would not even eat because the teasing was overwhelming. Instead, we would stuff our pita bread sandwiches in our pockets and bring them home after school. On other days, we would go home for lunch. This was much more comfortable for us, although we only had a thirty-minute lunch period. That meant we only had enough time to sprint home, eat like wolves, and sprint back.

Most kids thought we were Mexican and couldn't understand why we never spoke Spanish. Others thought we were Italian and called us micks or dagos. One kid thought I was from Africa, which was at least a *little* closer to my ancestral home, while another kid asked me if I was an Aborigine. I didn't even know what an Aborigine was at the time.

The truth is, we were all from somewhere else. It seemed like nearly everyone in our school was from Italy, Germany, Ireland, Mexico—you name it. And despite what modern sociologists say about how sensitive young children are, it's a fact that kids tease each other in school. It just happens. It's part of growing up. It's neither good nor bad. I was teased because I was different, and

I'm sure I teased others. Remember when I told you about pulling my sister's bonnet off in class? Sometimes we tease when we don't even try. I would be guilty of this on the first day of my junior year in high school.

We had finished our summer break; it had been a profitable one for our family. We even had enough money for me to get a gently worn pair of shoes. The summer had been rainy, and Mother was tired of me coming home with wet feet because of the holes in the soles of my shoes. In past years, I had gone to school without shoes or with shoes so worn I had to cover the holes in the bottom with cardboard.

The first day of school was mild, which is unusual for early September in Houston, and I decided to sit in the front row voluntarily. I was going to end up there anyway. When you have a last name that starts with *Ab*, you get used to sitting in the front. When the teacher came in, we all stood. She called our names, and we took our seats, alphabetically from the front row to the back row. I was number one, as usual. When the teacher got to F, she announced, "Fortenberry. Ruby Fortenberry."

I looked up, and Ruby was taking the seat next to me, one row over. As the name Fortenberry resonated in my head, it sounded like "Fart-in-berry." In our house, we never used the word *fart*. It wasn't proper. To hear the word in a classroom and spoken by the teacher was more than I could stand. I tried to hold back my laughter, but eventually I began to shake.

It wasn't long before our teacher, Mrs. Bemus, noticed my quivering and gave me the evil eye. I did my best to stop and succeeded for a while, until she recited the name again. I burst out with laughter. I got the evil eye again, but it didn't do any good this time, either. I was sent out into the hallway to "gather my composure." I did as she commanded, standing in the hall just outside the door and watching through the window as the class was seated one by one.

I tried to reenter the classroom three times, but each time I did, the name Fart-in-berry rang out in my head, and I began to laugh uncontrollably again. Each time it happened, I stopped dead in my tracks and looked over to Mrs. Bemus, who was scowling and pointing toward the door. So, I reversed my course and returned to my hallway detention.

Unfortunately for Ruby, my amusement with her name was somewhat contagious, and each time I peered through the glass on the upper part of the door or attempted to take my seat, the class joined in my laughter. Needless to say, I was not able to return to my seat that day and spent the entire period in the hallway.

I had to sit next to Ruby Fortenberry for the rest of that semester—or, I should say, she had to sit next to me. Notwithstanding my numerous apologies, she never spoke to me again. I didn't blame her.

We each have our little tortures in life, and mine happened that very same year in a different classroom. We were seated alphabetically as usual, and by some strange quirk of fate I was assigned the desk next to Jane Christine, the most beautiful creature I had ever seen in my life. I remember thinking even her name was pretty. She was exquisite, with long, brown hair and a classic Coca-Cola bottle figure.

My torture was not that she would not talk to me, but that I could not talk to *her*. She was a popular cheerleader, while I was merely a student, and the only extracurricular activities I took part in were my various jobs. I was also painfully shy, so much so that I couldn't muster the courage to form one word in her presence. Even when she would look at me from across the aisle, which was rare, I was unable to formulate even a single syllable. I was that tongue-tied. I could only look at her and wish. She really hung the moon for me.

Graduation from our small high school in North Houston was a mixed bag of emotions for me. Part of me was worried about what would come next. As a graduate, I would have a bigger responsibility to support my family. Another part of me was overjoyed at completing my primary education. To make it sweeter, my dear sister Juliette and I graduated only a semester apart due to her illness. She was handed her diploma in May 1940, while I walked in the graduation ceremony at Jefferson Davis High School in January 1941. High school only went to eleventh grade in those days.

Armed with a bona fide high school diploma, I set my sights on a regular job. After all, I no longer had to spend my days in the classroom. And although the *Chronicle* had declared me "Most Likely to Attend College," I felt my time was best spent working and supporting my family.

After graduation, two things attracted my attention: managing money and selling real estate. I ended up splitting my time between them. I also kept my paper route, as it was something I could do after I finished my day's work.

The first of my daytime jobs was at the bank, and my second

job was at Houston Title Company. I would like to tell you that I was a loan officer or even a teller at the bank, but the truth is I started out as a bank courier—a delivery boy with a title. It did, however, provide regular hours and a regular paycheck. My job at the title company was similar.

Before long, it became apparent I could not satisfy both my bosses. Their demands on my time were increasing as they gained confidence in me. The bank was interesting to me, and I loved trotting around town with cashier's checks bearing numbers I could not even imagine.

I remember standing by the teller as he cashed out his drawer. When he placed a bill in front of me, my eyes bulged until they hurt. There lay a thousand-dollar bill. *A thousand-dollar bill*! It was more money than I had made in my entire life, and it was sitting in one bill on the counter. In 1941, $1,000 was enough money to buy our two-bedroom house on Freeman Street. The U.S. Treasury no longer prints thousand-dollar bills, but that particular one is etched into my memory forever.

Ultimately, I ended up choosing the job at the title company for a pragmatic reason: the title company paid more. Despite my awe at the size of the cashier's checks and the allure of all the cash at the bank, the title company offered more opportunity, as I could learn how real estate was bought and sold. My father always dreamed of owning property.

He would tell me, "Investing in land is a sure thing. You can build an empire owning property. Buildings can be built, stores can be leased, and you are the holding the key: the land."

The hard part in those days was earning enough money to purchase the property or even make a down payment. Getting a loan was not easy either. During the Great Depression, money was tight. Despite the hurdles, my father's dream of owning real estate became mine.

My courier role at the title company soon blossomed into something more. I was asked to retrieve records from the courthouse. I didn't know where to start, but I was a quick study. At the courthouse, I learned how land ownership was recorded and how property liens were kept. And eventually a truly wonderful thing happened—I was asked to sit in on a closing. I jumped at the chance.

The closing room held a mystical appeal for me. It was a huge, dark, paneled room with a large oval mahogany table and a mass of highbacked, dark leather chairs. The closer sat at the head, the sellers sat on the left, and the buyers sat on the right. I couldn't believe how many papers were exchanged and how many signatures were required. Finally, there was the transfer of funds. Today, this is all done by wire transfer, but back when everything was signed in person, the buyer handed a cashier's check to the seller. I'd seen those checks during my time at the bank, but now they had new meaning.

I had gone from courier, to the courthouse, to the closing room. To put it simply, I was hooked. I saw this as my opportunity to learn, to prosper, and to lift my family out of financial peril. I had found my life's work and my future in real estate. Little did I know that my dreams would soon be interrupted, and my life would take a drastic detour when on December 7, 1941—a day that will truly live in infamy—the Japanese attacked us at Pearl Harbor.

WAR

For me and the United States, December 7, 1941, was monumental. It changed my world forever. In some ways, it seems like yesterday. I can still remember my family huddled around our small RCA radio, which was powered by vacuum tubes. As the words blared out of the oval wooden box, my usually loud, chattering family was stunned in disbelief. The silence was deafening. My God, our country was at war!

Had I been of age, I would have joined up the very next day, as so many did. As fate would have it, though, when the bombs dropped on Pearl Harbor, I was nine months shy of my eighteenth birthday. I thought of trying to lie my way into one of the branches of the military, but I knew they'd turned me away. I wanted to serve my country, but also knew my family needed me. I was still the major wage earner.

The war changed almost everything overnight. A country and an economy in the deep throes of depression suddenly turned on a dime and started producing anything and everything it needed to win the war. To win was the goal. It was not to reach a stalemate or to manage a police action. Our goal in World War II was to defeat the enemy and obtain unconditional surrender. There was no in-between, and there was no contemplation of losing.

Despite a decade of economic malaise, ours was still the best, most productive society on Earth, and we were ready to prove ourselves. We were also just a little angry about being sucker punched by the Japs. We wanted payback. Yes, you heard me right. We wanted *payback* and we made no bones about it. I didn't see anything wrong with it then and I don't see anything wrong with it today. If someone attacks you without warning—or even with warning, for that matter—you deserve retribution.

On Monday morning, December 8, 1941, lines at the induction offices went around the block. In those days, people knew their duty. Years later, I reflected on that moment while watching street riots and hearing stories of young men fleeing to Canada to avoid the draft.

I know the Vietnam War and World War II were very different wars. When I examine them closely with my aged eyes, I think it is a difference of confidence. You see, in the latter days of 1941, we all believed. We believed in our country, our leaders, and each other. By the time we made it to Southeast Asia, much of that confidence and trust had dissolved. And although I can see how the youth of this country has become disillusioned with the politicians, I still cannot and never will understand how they could possibly turn their backs on their country.

This country, this plot of land, is the only island of freedom left on the planet. It is fragile. I saw just how fragile during my time in the war. Perhaps that is one of the other differences between then and now. Back then I knew, as did many others, that we could lose the war against the Axis powers. They were a real and tangible threat. Our country had been bombed and it scared the hell out of me. I don't know if those who escaped their duty by crossing our northern border ever knew that fear. I sincerely hope if they ever do feel it, they will come to the rescue of the most beautiful of women: Liberty.

In 1941, it seemed as if every man who could fight signed up for World War II and was off to boot camp in a matter of weeks. The rest of us who were left behind knew we also had a duty to perform. We were certainly not going to fail in our support of the war effort.

Uncle William, my mentor, came to the rescue again by finding both of us jobs at the shipyard. This was our way of contributing. Months earlier, the shipyard was a meagerly used stretch of land along the Houston Ship Channel. It was now transformed into a veritable beehive of activity. America needed ships of all kinds—warships, merchant vessels, everything imaginable—and every shipyard in the country sprang into action.

I had no construction skills, but I wanted to work and do my part. I ended up painting ships. I would like to tell you I painted the outside of some grand warship, but my job was to slop red primer on the cargo holds of merchant vessels that were being refurbished. The work was hard, and the old hands—the ones who had been at the shipyard for years—couldn't resist having a little fun with all of us youngsters. God, I must have looked like such a kid. I was tall, lanky, and had innocence smeared all over my face, alongside splatters of that iridescent red-orange primer.

The old boys would set me up with what I needed first thing in the morning and send me on my way. In all honesty, I think they were a little jealous of my youth. I could work all day and not get tired. After a few days of priming the interior bulkheads of a medium-size tanker, Roy, the oldest of the old-timers, set me to the task of priming an overhang. I found out quickly this is the ceiling of a ship. I took to my task with the same exuberance as always, but this time the old-timers stuck around and watched. This made me nervous, of course. They hadn't watched me work since I'd arrived many weeks earlier. I could feel their eyes on me as I took my brush and carefully spread the viscous liquid on the metal plate overhead.

They started giving me instructions.

"Ya gotta put it on thicker, boy. Get your brush full of paint and really slop it on."

My first reaction was to think they were asking me to waste paint. I grew up conserving everything, but they were the bosses and I was the green kid. Our roles were established from the very beginning, so I did as they instructed and slopped on more primer. With each brushstroke, they demanded I layer it on thicker and thicker. What I didn't notice was that while I was concentrating on doing my duty to their satisfaction, they were busy painting my shoes.

It wasn't until I dunked my brush in the bucket for what seemed like the fortieth time that I saw that my shoes were a familiar red-orange color. I must have paused for a full thirty seconds in confusion. When I finally looked up at Roy and his accomplice, they burst into laughter so loud I could hardly hear myself think.

"Look at you, boy! You really look like a painter now," they cackled.

I stopped and looked at my shoes and then at those old men

Ralph in uniform as a member of the US Army Air Force during WWII.

with gnarly brown teeth, and I couldn't help but laugh with them. It was all part of my education.

When I went outside to get air, Uncle William walked by and saw me.

"What the hell happened to you, Ralph?" he asked.

"Oh, you mean my shoes?" I replied.

Uncle William looked at my feet and snickered. Painting the new guy's shoes was an old joke at the shipyard.

"It's not only your shoes, Ralph. You need to look in the mirror," he looked at me and said, grinning.

As I opened the door to the head (a bathroom on a ship) and saw my reflection, I nearly fainted. My face and hair were the color of my shoes. I quickly realized the demands of the old men to slop more and more paint on the overhang had all been part of the joke.

I spent the spring and summer of 1942 at the shipyard. I never missed a day of work, even though at times I wanted to. It was grueling work and stiflingly hot in the unventilated cargo holds, but that was okay. Everyone else had to sacrifice, and so did I.

My time at the shipyard went quickly, and before I knew it, it was August 24, 1942—my eighteenth birthday. Early that morning, I stood outside the induction office and waited to register to serve my country. Although I was ready, they were not. To my dismay and embarrassment, I was sent home to wait for my draft notice, which came the following week. I read it eagerly and saw I was ranked 1-C, which meant I wasn't leaving immediately. My mother was sad and worried, but I was anxious to go, fight, and do my duty. I went back to work in the shipyard for what seemed like an eternity, though it was only six months.

Finally, in February 1943, I was called to serve in the United States Army Air Force. I was thrilled.

MOTHER LOOKED AT ME WITH DIFFERENT EYES

The floor of the induction center was covered with ice-cold green tile, but the excitement in the building was electric. Perhaps we were just young, stupid kids, but we all knew we were at the beginning of a great adventure whose outcome was uncertain.

We were all so eager to defend our country.

Having seldom been out of the confines of Houston, Texas, I was more than just a little overwhelmed by it all. I was eighteen, 125 pounds on a good day, and the son of Lebanese immigrants. But above all, I was an American—American born and American through and through. Standing in our skivvies in a cold room and waiting to turn our heads and cough, we soon learned we were all the same.

At Fort Hood, we were inoculated not only from any disease we might catch overseas but also from civilian life. Our sergeant showed us the virtues of military organization and accountability. We were only there for a few days before being cattle carried to

Clearwater, Florida, which was twenty hours of sitting in our seats and listening to the *clickety-clack* of steel wheels on iron rails. The seats were lumpy and hard, but that didn't matter. I was way too keyed up to sleep. We all were.

Basic training was what I expected. We learned to march in cadence and shoot rifles and pistols. We learned the absolute necessity of following orders. No lesson was more important. Orders woke us up in the morning and tucked us in at night.

For some, the regiment of army life was a strain, but in some ways for me, it was both a pleasure and a relief from my youth. For one thing, we had three square meals a day. This was much more food than I was used to. And we were outside marching and singing most of the time—a far cry from nearly suffocating in the holds of old ships, choking on the fumes of lead-based, red-orange primer. And although most recruits complained about the cots we slept on, I did not. My days in the army were the first time I had a bed to sleep on.

I remember feeling a bit intimidated the first day or two of boot camp, but by the time we were ready to ship out, I had gained my confidence. The skin on the back of my neck, which had been white and exposed from the barber's clippers at the beginning of boot camp, was now tanned. I could see the new recruits looking enviously at me out of the corners of their eyes, and I remembered doing the same thing when I'd first arrived. The real telltale signs were the stripes on our arms. You didn't get those until the end of boot camp after you graduated, and they looked really good. Most of us got a simple chevron, signifying the rank of private. A few got an added rocker and the title "private first class" for finishing top in their company. That rank was a little extra, but all of us still had to take orders from the sergeants, who were there to be obeyed.

The stripes on our shoulders were still brand new when we heard about our convoy. We would leave out of lovely New Jersey, but not for a few weeks. We were staged like spare parts at a little camp in Hattiesburg, Mississippi. This was just another delay on the way to the war.

Staging for deployment is a lonely and boring task. The sergeants did their best to keep us occupied, but we were just out of basic training and tired of drill. You can only march a soldier so much. We all had our jobs, and we all lived in pup tents. The days dragged on, and it wasn't uncommon to see groups of young men standing together, often talking about what might come next or talking about home. I couldn't help but have the same thoughts. I was both excited and scared to go overseas. I wanted to do my patriotic duty, but I was also missing home. Having never been away from my family before, I didn't know what comfort and support they afforded me until then.

The days were all beginning to meld together when our sergeant mustered us in the platoon area one afternoon and announced we would all be given a forty-eight-hour pass. He added that we needed to return on time and sober. This was never an issue for me. In my eighteen years, I never had a drink.

Although the sergeant never said so, we all knew this would be our last taste of liberty before we shipped out. Many of the soldiers in my platoon started making plans immediately. Some set their sights on New Orleans, Bourbon Street, and anything and everything that might come from there. After all, we had been confined to base for six weeks. What popped into my head was that Hattiesburg, Mississippi, was a mere twelve-hour drive from my home in Houston. I didn't have a car—none of us did—but I had heard hitchhiking had become popular with soldiers, and I was game to try.

At 6:45 a.m. on a Friday morning, just after breakfast, I set out to find my home and family. I was armed with a small bag containing a change of clothes, a shaving kit, and $4.32 in my pocket. I sent most of my army pay home, but now I wished I'd saved a few extra dollars for a bus ticket.

My only other asset was my thumb. I stood on the side of the road and held out my arm as my tent mates had instructed. Lo and behold, the fourth car to pass slowed and stopped not twenty yards from where I stood. I ran to the car with excitement and peered into the four-door sedan. Inside was a family—Dad behind the wheel, Mom in the passenger seat, and their two young boys in the back. As I stared at the boys, they stared back at me with gaping mouths. I don't think they had ever been this close to a real soldier before.

"We're going as far as New Orleans," the man said.

I nodded and opened the back door. The boys slid to the far side of the bench seat. I got in.

We started on our journey. The woman asked the polite questions that all well-bred women ask.

"Where are you from?"

"Are you going home?"

"Does your family know you're coming?"

I answered in short, polite sentences.

"I'm from Houston," I said.

"Yes, I'm going home on a forty-eight-hour leave."

"No, I thought it would be better to surprise them," I concluded.

I was new to this kind of encounter.

I tried to ignore the boys' eyes boring in on me, but I couldn't. Their stares were too intense. Finally, I faced them and smiled. That was all it took. The floodgates opened, and those two little boys asked me every question that was rattling around in their heads.

"How many Japanese have you killed?" they asked first.

"None, so far," I answered.

I could tell this disappointed them.

"But I hope to go to Europe and kill Germans," I offered.

They immediately giggled, made guns out of their hands, and proceeded to shoot at everything in the car. The ride to New Orleans went quickly after that, and I couldn't help but enjoy the attention of those two young boys. I felt like a celebrity.

They let me out at the intersection of Interstate 10 and the Pontchartrain Expressway before heading south to Belle Chasse. My route was west to Houston. I waved goodbye; the boys waved through the back window as the family sped away.

Once again, I stood on the side of the freeway with my thumb out. I hoped and prayed I would be picked up soon. My prayers were answered in only a few minutes. This time it was a truck. *Thank God he stopped*, I thought. I ran to the passenger side, reached up, and popped open the door. I pulled myself up, threw my bag on the floor, and thanked the driver for stopping. To my shock, it was a woman. I was taken aback for a moment. Then I thanked *her* for stopping.

"I know, a woman driving a grocery truck. Not what you expected," she said.

"No, ma'am, not at all what I was expecting, but we didn't expect the Japs to attack our country either," I replied.

She agreed and asked where I was headed.

"Houston," I said.

"This is your lucky day, soldier. That is just where I'm going."

Over the next eight hours she told me about her husband, who had joined up the day after Pearl Harbor. He was so brave, and she was so proud. He had left her and their two children to defend our country. Not long after boot camp, he shipped out to the Pacific Theater. He ended up in a reinforcement platoon on Corregidor Island just before it was overrun by the Japanese and died somewhere on the forced march to Balanga, the capital of Bataan. She said the letter from the War Department indicated he died valiantly.

We both had read about the Bataan Death March—an unconscionable, brutal affair—in the papers. As they had marched and marched, our soldiers had been beaten, bayoneted, starved, and given nothing to drink except water from filthy water buffalo wallows on the side of the road. At times, our soldiers had been forced to bury their comrades alive; any refusal had resulted in samurai-style execution. At any sign of dissension, the Japanese would line up our soldiers, draw their swords, and behead those they thought were leaders, while the rest of our troops could only watch in horror. I don't think most Americans knew until then just how vicious and cruel the Japanese army could be. We would learn many more lessons over the course of the war.

Tears rolled down the driver's face as she told me her husband's story. Her pride in him was contagious, and I found myself wanting to return to my unit as soon as my leave was over so that I too could do *my* duty. We both wept for her loss, for our country, and for our fragile future.

She dropped me off only a block from my house, even though it was far out of her way. I realized this woman was a hero just like her husband. She did everything she could to keep the wheels of industry and liberty churning. She filled the void inside herself and our country with work, pride, and dignity.

It was 6 p.m. when I stood in front of our house. The evening light from the setting sun still illuminated the porch of our tiny square box on Freeman Street. I had always known it was a humble house, but this was the first time I saw just how humble. When I was a child, it had been adequate. We were all able to live under its roof and it was all we knew. Now, looking at this meager two-bedroom house, I found it hard to imagine how we had all fit in there. Standing on the street and seeing it through new eyes, I realized our tiny house was only slightly more than a shack.

I approached the porch, and a strange man opened the front door.

"May I help you, soldier?" he said.

May I help you? I thought. *This is my house. What are you doing here?*

"I am looking for my family, who lives here," I replied.

"You must be Ralph," the man said, smiling.

I was taken aback. How did he know my name and why was he standing in the doorway of my home?

"Yes, sir, I am Ralph. May I ask your name, sir?"

"I am Charles. Your family moved last week—one block over to Everett Street."

"You're kidding," I replied. "Moved?"

I made my way around the block and stood looking in awe at the second house on the left. There I saw my brothers Louis, Jack, and George playing on the porch. My first reaction was disbelief. This was such a large house—thin and long like one of those shotgun houses in New Orleans. I made my way down the street, stood in front of the house, and yelled to my brothers. They stood stunned, unable to move. At first, they looked at me as if I were a total stranger. I knew I looked different. Boot camp transforms almost everyone. And, of course, there was the uniform. They had seen plenty of uniforms before, but they had never seen one on me. At last, they recognized me. It seemed to come to all three of them at the same time.

"Is that you, brother? Is that really you?" Louis screamed.

"It can't be! No way! But it is!" yelled George.

"Yes. It is me, my brothers!" I exclaimed.

All three leaped off the porch and raced toward me. It was like being hit by a wave. They all hugged me at once.

"Have you won the war already, Ralph?" questioned Jack, the youngest.

"How long will you stay?" asked Louis.

There were so many questions I couldn't begin to answer them all. My brothers were running in circles like puppy dogs at play. I loved every second of their embrace and love. Despite all the excitement at seeing my brothers, I heard the screen door slam shut on the porch. I turned my head, and my eyes beheld a most heavenly sight. Mother and Juliette were standing on the porch, having heard all the commotion. They stood frozen as they looked out into the yard at the lanky soldier who was staring back at them. Breaking free from my brothers, I raced to my mother and held both her and Juliette tight. The wooden spoon and potholder they were holding now lay on the porch. Tears ran down our faces.

I had seen my mother cry many times, but this was the first time I had seen her cry tears of joy.

"Is it you, Ralph? Is it really you?"

My mother wept. Juliette, who was still stunned, could only hold on to my arm that was wrapped around her.

"Yes, Mother. It's me," I whispered in her ear tenderly.

For a moment I could feel the two of them shake gently as tears filled their eyes and streaked down their cheeks. I cannot remember a more tender moment in my entire life.

My brothers broke the moment, rushing to the house and vaulting the three steps to the porch. There, we all hugged each other as if this was the last time we may all be together.

We finally untangled, and my dear mother stood squarely in front of me, held her arms out, took me by the hands, and said, "Let me look at you, Ralph. Let me just look at you. My goodness, you've grown into a man. My little boy is now a man!"

I told her I was only there for the night and had to return to base the next afternoon. Our company would likely be shipped out to England within the next few days. None of that made any difference to her. She was just happy to see me.

Mother looked at me with different eyes that day. I felt the same and I thought I looked the same, but the expression on her face told me I didn't. I thought maybe it was the uniform, the shiny brass buckle, and the stripe on my sleeve—I even had a National Defense Service Medal to show off—but I realized it wasn't my clothes. I had changed. I was no longer a boy in my mother's eyes. I was a man.

I thought I became a man the night I confronted my father and found that lone penny in the grass. I may have looked like a boy, but I had behaved like a man from that moment forward. I had not shirked my obligations, I had embraced them, made sacrifices, and never complained. However, I realize now what I saw in my mother's eyes that day on the porch was pride, not only in the little boy selling goods on the street, but in the man who had stepped up to defend his country.

My family couldn't wait to take me on a tour of the new house. I was thrilled. It had three bedrooms, a living room, a dining room, a large den, and a kitchen that was as big as half of our old house. It was the biggest house I had ever been in. As I looked around, I realized that someone was missing.

"Where is Johnnie?" I asked.

My mother was about to explain when I heard the cry from the front door.

"Brother, is that you? Really, is that you, Ralph?"

I walked to the front of the house and grabbed him in a bear hug. The smiles on our faces touched our ears. We ended up sitting around the dining room table, talking, eating, and talking some more. At the Freeman Street house, we put a board between two chairs to create enough seats for us all to eat together. Not here. The table was much bigger. A large piece of plywood balanced on an unstable four-legged frame, covered by a handmade tablecloth from the old country. And surrounding it were eight rickety chairs that came from disparate homes. But for us it was a magnificent arrangement, fit for a queen and her family. For the first time in our lives, we all had a place at the table.

Mother put her sweets out for us. They were like no other and they melted in our mouths. Mom was so excited that every time my plate was empty, she filled it up again.

"No more," I told her, but my plea fell on deaf ears.

Everything was so different. There was an abundance of food on the table, a bed for everyone to sleep on, and a large house to get lost in. Everyone had grown up, too. I think the whole country grew up that year.

We talked late into the night. Mom told me the story of how she'd bought the house. It sounds so silly, but the money she'd saved in mason jars in the kitchen on Freeman Street finally added up. Not long after I left for boot camp, she went to the bank and made the down payment. The house cost $3,000, and her down payment was $300. It had taken her twelve years to save that much.

After only a few hours of sleep, I woke in the boys' room just before dawn. Through the window, I saw the eastern sky turn from black to gray to a light shade of pink. I lay back on the pillow and looked at Johnnie lying on the floor beside me, just as we slept at the Freeman Street house, growing up. The difference was he had a blanket instead of newspapers to keep him warm. Before Jack, George, and Louis woke, Johnnie asked me about the army. I could tell he was making plans for his own enlistment. His eighteenth birthday was coming up soon and he'd already been to see the navy and wanted to know what I thought.

Somehow my six months in the army had made me an expert on the military. I told him stories of boot camp, the people I met, and the places I had been. I talked about where I suspected I was going next. Of course, I wanted him to join the army so we could be together, but he had his heart set on the navy, so I told him that was where he needed to be.

Mom let me sleep in. The smell of her bread woke me up as

it had so many times when I was a child. It took me a moment to remember where I was. I looked on the floor where Johnnie should have been, but he was gone. He had picked up a morning paper route to supplement his job at the shipyard.

I entered the kitchen and saw my mother standing near the oven and smiling. She was different—calm and somehow satisfied.

When Johnnie returned, we walked the entire neighborhood. Louis, Jack, and George joined us. I think they wanted to show me off. It was as if I'd never existed before then. They actually introduced me to our old friends. They even told me about the street we now lived on as if it were unknown to me, though it was only a block from where we all had grown up. I found out then just how powerful a uniform can be.

We had an early dinner that evening, since I had to be on the road by 6 p.m. to make it back to the base on time. I had originally planned on hitchhiking again, but Mother wouldn't hear of it. She reached into her cache of money and handed me enough for bus fare. She said she couldn't bear the thought of me on the side of the highway, as it reminded her of that awful night on the way back from Elgin.

I thought of telling her I had been through much worse than that night, but she didn't need to hear that, as it would only make her feel guilty. She had done the best she could. Everyone in the family had a good-paying job, and she had such a loyal following for her bread that people actually complained if she didn't bake for a day or two.

Our meal that day was a true celebration. My mother cooked all morning and even invited friends from church, which was a treat, as we rarely invited guests for dinner. The table was filled with all our favorite foods: hummus, baba ghanoush, kibbeh, grape leaves, and even stuffed squash. It was a feast.

This was a far cry from the home that I'd left only a few months earlier. I knew we didn't suddenly get rich; the signs of our poverty were still apparent. I just think my mother wanted to show me they were okay—that I didn't have to worry about them.

The bus station was crowded that night. My family escorted me through the terminal like a group of Secret Service agents. I got a window seat, and I still remember my brothers running alongside, waving and yelling as the bus pulled out of the station. I suppose another person might have been embarrassed, but I wasn't. They were my family, and I loved them.

NOT THE JOB I EXPECTED

I took the last bus I could, and I would have arrived at the base in plenty of time if the bus had not broken down outside of Lake Charles, Louisiana. The delay made me two hours late. When I arrived at the base, the sergeant met me, called me into his tent, and chewed me out the way only army sergeants can. I felt so low, like I had let myself and my unit down. As a punishment, I was restricted to camp the night before we shipped out.

Everybody else went to town but me. I know my sergeant didn't really want to do it—I could see the empathy in his eyes—but he had to. Discipline is the cornerstone of any army. In retrospect, my punishment was mild. I certainly had not planned to return to the base late; however, I knew going to Houston had risks. It was worth it to see my family.

Reveille woke us at 5 a.m. and our mission began. Our first leg was the twenty-four-hour trip from Mississippi to the New Jersey docks. Soldiers filled the train. It was standing room only. We were all excited to finally get to the war, but lingering under the surface were the doubts of all young men in our position. This was why we had enlisted, and this is what we had trained for. I don't think I slept a wink. I don't think any of us did. We wrote to our families, played cards, and smoked. We did anything to pass the time.

Our train arrived in New Jersey late that night. The trainyard was not far from the harbor. Clouds of steam from the train bellowed over the water and the ships. The picture was surreal. Soldiers with heavy packs exited the train, mustered into company formation, and marched toward the ships. The white smoke was so thick it was hard to see. The quiet and stillness were chilling. No one spoke; we just did what we were told. We marched, unit by unit, across the tracks. After trekking less than half a mile, we saw the docks.

The harbor was full of ships. I had never seen anything like it in my life. The vessels I helped paint in Houston were tiny compared to these. The closer we got, the bigger they were. When we reached dockside, we had to look nearly straight up to see the smokestacks of the transports. I was in awe. I couldn't believe anything was so enormous.

We boarded via the gangplank. Our hearts beat like drums as we took turns filing onto the ship, unit after unit made up of soldiers carrying packs nearly double their size.

The mighty *Orion* was our ride to England. She was a merchant vessel with a crew from India. Our company ended up in the bowels of the ship. When we finally arrived at our quarters, we found they contained no beds. Instead, our rooms were filled with hammocks. Some soldiers never got the hang of swaying to and fro, so they ended up sleeping on the floor.

We had only been in our new home for a short time when I realized our quarters were below the waterline. I heard the propellers churn the water and the metal hull creak and pop under the strain of the cargo as it was being loaded. Having only a sheet of iron between me and the icy waters of the North Atlantic was unnerving when we were in port, and it was worse when we were out at sea.

The *Orion* was one of many ships in our convoy. Our flagship was the battleship *Texas*. For nearly two weeks, we rolled and pitched on the gray-green waters of the North Atlantic. At first, I was hardly able to get into my hammock; it was so small. When I finally got in, I flipped right out of it. Each night, it took several tries to balance my body in this swaying thing the navy called a bed. As difficult as it was, I had it pretty good compared to others. When I finally made it up on deck, I saw some of the soldiers had no beds at all and had to endure the trip across the Atlantic topside. Relative to that, my little hammock seemed like a luxury.

As I walked around the deck, I was amazed by everyone's spirit. Even though they had to make the voyage exposed to the elements with little protection, they did not complain. Instead, they filled the time by playing cards, throwing dice, and, of course, talking about everything in the world—the war, their families, and their girlfriends back home. That was the attitude of our country in those days. You simply made the best of the situation at hand.

During the entire trip I saw those men worry only once when general quarters was sounded. Everyone on board was apprehensive that day. One of the ships in the convoy had detected a submarine. The German wolfpacks sunk many ships over the course of the war and we wondered if we would be their next victim.

When the sirens rang out, there was a mad flurry of activity. Crew members raced to their duty stations and soldiers went to their bunks. Everyone had a place. Mine was with my company twelve feet below the waterline. We could all feel the ship as it turned back and forth in a zigzag pattern, making it hard for a U-boat to hit us with a torpedo. We all waited in silence, listening to the massive propellers cut through the water and the sonar ping. I was thankful I joined the army and not the navy. I couldn't help but think of my brother Johnnie and what he might face when he finally became a seaman. I missed him terribly. I took a moment and said a prayer for him and the rest of my family.

We secured from general quarters only an hour or so after it was sounded. I don't know if we evaded the U-boat, or if it was only a false alarm, but no ships were sunk or fired upon and we made it to the port of Liverpool, England, without incident. We all felt blessed.

I had heard the port of Liverpool was one of the largest in the world. I'm sure the war made it even larger. The amount of activity in that relatively small area was mind-boggling. We had just watched the whitecaps on the Atlantic for days, and now all we could see was an ocean of drab olive green. There was machinery everywhere we looked—tanks, trucks, guns. In and around all of it were thousands of soldiers.

Despite all the equipment and assistance supplied to this small island nation, Jolly Ole' England wasn't so jolly. Air raids still occurred; the German V-1 Buzz Bombs and V-2 rockets were an everyday presence. By this stage of the war, Hitler was killing more British civilians than British military.

After assembling onshore, we were loaded onto trucks and

convoyed first to Manchester, then to Molesworth Royal Air Force Base. We rode huddled together in open-topped trucks. The air was icy cold and thick with moisture. It was like driving through a cloud. This would be my lasting impression of England.

When we reached Molesworth, we gladly jumped down from the trucks and found our quarters. The barracks were little more than hastily constructed wooden boxes, but they would provide shelter from the rain and chilling wind. This would be my home for the next twenty-two months.

We had been at the airfield for less than an hour when we heard the call of the air-raid siren. We hadn't even unpacked our gear—what a welcome! I'll never forget the whining siren. Not knowing what to do, we simply followed everyone else, who headed for the bunkers. Safely inside, we could hear the distinctive rumble of the Buzz Bomb. This was my first experience with the V-1 rocket, and I grew to fear and loathe its sound. It was also my first contact with the German war machine, which represented tyranny and oppression. It was everything I had come here to fight against.

Shortly after a distant explosion, the all clear was sounded. I was thankful the V-1s were not very accurate. This one had ended up detonating in a nearby field, so there were no casualties or damage.

We learned many of the activities at the base the same way we learned where to go during an air raid—we simply followed everyone else. I discovered that even in war, there is a rhythm and a ritual to life. Ours was centered on the squadron of B-17 Flying Fortresses we were there to support. Our schedule revolved around their sorties. We gathered early in the morning just after dawn and prepped the planes for their mission. We loaded the bombs into the bellies of the aircraft, then helped the crew into their fleece-lined clothing as they boarded. The fuselage of the B-17 was not pressurized, and at 15,000 feet the temperature dropped to twenty below zero. We stood and watched as the lumbering creatures took flight and joined their formation. Shoulder-to-shoulder in silence, we counted the planes as they took off.

After the planes were out of sight, we went about our daily duties until they returned. We heard them long before we saw them. A squadron of B-17s made a low rumble I learned to recognize anywhere.

The most severely damaged planes were the first to land. If radio contact was not possible because it was shot up during the mission, the crews used flares to communicate. Red flares were the worst. They meant the plane had wounded aboard. White flares meant the aircraft was low on fuel and needed to come in quickly. Bombers with landing-gear problems had to wait until last. We couldn't risk the possibility of the gear collapsing and the plane blocking the runway.

We counted the planes as they flew over and compared it to our count from that morning. It was a good day when the numbers matched, but there were not many good days. We Americans had taken on the unenviable task of daytime bombing. Bombers could be more accurate in the daytime, but their missions were much more dangerous. The Luftwaffe had been weakened, but it had by no means been defeated. Our daylight raids were taking a toll on the Germans' infrastructure, and they knew it. Their fighters were their only defense, and they knew that too. As a result, their pilots fought devilishly hard.

When each of our planes landed, the support crews rushed

in to help. As we ran to the hatches, we couldn't help but notice the bullet holes and the tattered rudders, wings, and ailerons. The crews who exited the plane were never concerned about themselves; their first thoughts were always for their wounded. As they handed the broken bodies of their crewmates out of the hatches, they yelled for the stretchers. That's where we came in.

My team arrived with makeshift litters—two poles with a blanket stretched between them. We carried the men to waiting jeeps, straddled the stretchers across the front and back, and started our slow roll to the field hospital. The whole process was controlled chaos. Movement and noise were everywhere. Men were running from one plane to another. And over it all, we could hear the cries of the wounded and the anguished.

Once we delivered the stretchers and the medics rendered first aid, we returned to the tarmac to help with the next landed bomber. We repeated this cycle until all the planes that were coming back had landed. Sometimes, a badly damaged plane that had lost an engine was slow to return. It would appear on the horizon, and touch down to the cheers of us all. This didn't happen often, but it did happen, so we always waited and hoped. When hope is all you have, hope is what you cling to.

When enough time had passed, we knew there would be no more planes, but we waited a little longer just the same. Finally, we returned to our barracks to hear what we could about the mission. We always wanted to ask about what happened even though we usually knew. It was written on the faces of the pilots and their crews.

When the squadron was finally accounted for, we did our best to help with the wounded and ready the planes for their next mission. We all had our duties—some of them good and some not so good. Not long after I arrived, I was assigned the job of driving the belongings of fallen soldiers from our base in Molesworth to London. From there, the belongings were loaded onto ships and ultimately delivered to the grieving families back home. The personal effects of each soldier would travel many legs before arriving at their destination. My part was to transport these items on the first leg of their trip.

Driving through the dense soupy fog was the most dangerous part of this gruesome detail. The fog was always there, morning or evening, but it was especially thick at night. And, of course, most of my trips were at night. That's just the way the schedule worked.

I had to collect the items and pack them. At first, I purposely ignored the pictures. I wrapped them quickly and securely, then tucked them away. I didn't feel like I had the right to look at them. I knew these men only for a short while. At the time, I felt like a thief going through someone else's things.

I carried out my duty as professionally and honorably as I could, but I would inevitably find myself staring at boxes of medals or photos of the fallen soldier's family. Looking back, I cannot believe how young they all were. I guess I was too, but for some reason when I looked at those pictures, I felt old in comparison. Nothing will age a person like dealing with death.

Some of their faces are still stuck in my mind today. They now appear to me like Norman Rockwell paintings, but that is how our entire country looked back then. I had not traveled before going to war, but looking at those pictures gave me a perspective on my own country that I never had before. I quickly came to realize we were a country of small-town farms, local shopkeepers, and close, loving families. In an odd way, I could see my own family in some of the images. Tall, thin boys, who could not fill out their shirts standing next to their parents—fathers with sinewy muscles and callused hands, mothers with careworn faces. Brothers and sisters wearing obvious hand-me-downs clinging to their older brothers' pant legs and staring at them with pride, admiration, and a hidden sense of fear. Would they ever come back?

I worked swiftly but took care to wrap and pack every item and every box to the best of my ability. Each family deserved to receive every remembrance in the condition I found it. The thought of having the glass in one picture frame break on its trek home was hateful to me. I was not putting my life on the line like these boys were, but I still had a job to do and I was bound and determined to do it right.

The boxes were always of different sizes. Some guys just had more stuff than others; it was not more complicated than that. I would stack the boxes by the barracks door before checking out a jeep from the motor pool and loading it up. As the afternoon hours wore on, I would get nervous and hurry the packing just a little more. Deep down I knew why. I'd never been a sneak, but I felt like one then.

One day, while on my despicable detail, I stacked the last box by the door and went back for something—I don't remember exactly what. What I do remember is the face of the man who entered the other end of the barracks just as I was getting ready to leave. He stood stone-cold still as he alternately looked at me and what was now his friend's empty bunk area. I wanted to reach out to him and tell him how sorry I was, but I couldn't. It wasn't my place. Soldiers have strange, unspoken protocols. In the end, I simply saluted and took the boxes out. The man at the other end of the long, thin building could only remove his cap and hang his head in sorrow. I have never seen a sadder sight in my life.

I loaded the jeep as precisely as I could and tried to fit as many boxes as possible, but space was limited. I was grateful the jeeps had canvas covers. It was always raining, and I didn't want the boxes or their contents to get wet.

With the jeep securely loaded, I took my final inventory and checked out at the main gate. The military police (MPs) verified the number of boxes and signed me out. I already let my sergeant know I was leaving on another trip, but I asked the MPs to call him before evening muster just to make sure he remembered. I didn't want to have a repeat of Mississippi. I try to learn lessons only once.

Starting out in the evening, I tried to get as far as I could before darkness fell. That's when things got dangerous. We were told never to use the headlights, during the day and especially at night. Blackout meant blackout, and even one careless act could give away our position to enemy aircraft visiting London and surrounding towns.

Even before sunset I found it difficult to see, partially because of the dim light, but mostly because of the fog, which we called "pea soup." Sometimes it was so thick I could hardly see the nose of the jeep. In addition to obscuring my view, the fog was damp and cold—the kind of cold that cuts through any coat and penetrates you to the core. I don't remember being so cold in my life. It got chilly in Houston, and we also had fog, but the fog in Houston was a sultry blanket that warmed and caressed you, nothing like this icy cold lady who seemed to breathe death down the back of your neck.

When the sun finally set, I felt the temperature drop. I pulled my coat tight around me, but it did little good. I drove as fast as I could, but I was limited to a snail's pace with no lights and all the fog. I didn't want to waste time, but I found myself inching along the narrow roads and almost feeling my way. I often heard the engines of other jeeps or trucks, but there was no way to know which direction the engine noise was coming from. I always imagined that a ten-ton truck was going to come out of the fog and crush me like a bug. The temptation to turn on the headlights, if only for a few seconds, was almost insurmountable. But the thought of my fellow soldiers in battle prevented me from doing so. If they could hold up under the strain of battle with death tugging at their elbows, I could certainly withstand this. I flinched when trucks came out of the fog unexpectedly. It was almost impossible not to. The key was to keep from jerking so hard that I ended up in a ditch. I had to protect my precious cargo.

I drove most of the night and would usually get to London just as the sun rose. The dome of St. Paul's Cathedral was a silhouette against the brightening sky. I had never seen anything so magnificent in my life. It was like something out of Dickens and the Bible all at the same time. Sometimes birds rose from the surrounding buildings and circled the spire of the cathedral dome. That's when I took a few moments to praise God for my life.

When my delivery was complete, I often reversed course and headed right back. On rare occasions, I would take the opportunity to visit a landmark in London. I'd never seen a city this old. Much

Ralph, in front on the far right, sporting a mustache, with his squadron in England at Molesworth Royal Air Force Base during WWII.

Ralph standing next to the "Flying Fortress" (B-17 bomber). These were the planes from which he assisted the wounded and respectfully carried the fallen soldiers.

Ralph with a compadre, posing by one of the many army jeeps he drove carrying the personal effects of the fallen soldiers from Molesworth Royal Air Force Base to Liverpool during WWII.

of Houston had been built in the 1920s and '30s. Several times, I made my way to St. Paul's on foot across the cobblestone streets.

After seeing it from afar, I felt I had to go inside. I always stopped and marveled at the architecture. It was so beautiful; I couldn't help but stare in awe. When I entered St. Paul's, the first thing I noticed was the smell of incense, which took me right back to Houston and the Orthodox services held in our homes. As I walked forward, I was truly cowed by the size and majesty of the interior. I took a few minutes and sat in a pew.

To this day, I cannot think of a better place to pray.

OFF TO BATTLE, ALMOST

In February or March of 1944 (I can't remember exactly when), the 303rd Bomber Group—of which I was a member—received a Distinguished Unit Citation for an operation that occurred on January 11, 1944. On that day, our unit successfully struck and destroyed an aircraft assembly plant in the German town of Oschersleben. In spite of continuous attacks by enemy fighters and a lack of Allied fighter support due to poor weather conditions, we still nailed the target. I distinctly remember the ceremony, mostly because it was attended by King George VI and his wife, the Queen Consort Elizabeth, and their daughters Princess Elizabeth (who would become queen) and Princess Margaret. General Jimmy Doolittle, one of the true heroes of World War II, was also in attendance.

I remember being so impressed at the sight of royalty. I'd never been so close to someone so famous. There was an aura about them. King George's stature and grace were mystifying. They had genuine smiles on their faces as they shook all our hands and thanked us for our service. I felt as if they were part of us, a group of human beings with the common goal to fight the oppression of

In 1945, the 303rd Squadron of the US Army Air Force receives the distinguished medal of honor from King George VI. Also greeting the servicemen are Queen Consort Elizabeth and Princess Elizabeth and Princess Margaret. Ralph was one of the many honored servicemen who can be seen in the background.

a man who embodied evil. They were so close I could hear them speak with their calm, confident voices. I grabbed my camera and began to take pictures. I knew this was history and I wanted to capture every second of it for myself and my family back home.

In contrast to the majesty of the royals, Jimmy Doolittle was like a little banty rooster. He was stout and he strutted with the air of a man who knew he could do just about anything. His raid on Tokyo not long after the Japanese attack on Pearl Harbor proved that he *could* do just about anything. I remember looking into his eyes for a brief moment as he passed. In that instant I saw the depth of the man, as well as his courage and determination. I couldn't help but wonder what those eyes had seen, and I have to admit I was a little jealous. I entered the war late. It was 1944 and I had not seen battle. I still wanted to do my part, no matter how terrifying it might be. And later that year, I had a chance to do what I joined up for.

It was December 1944, and we had all heard about Germany's winter offensive. It was a bold and desperate move by the Third Reich, and we were worried they just might succeed. There were rumors about the 101st Airborne being surrounded at Bastogne and refusing to surrender.

We continued our missions, which, we were told, were having their desired effect. The 303rd had progressed from bombing German-held sites in Holland and Belgium to being one of the first squadrons to drop bombs on German soil. We were finally reaching the homeland and destroying airplane factories, tank factories, and railway terminals. Yet, despite ours and the Allies' efforts, the German war machine was still rolling forth and there was a need for more infantry troops. Patton, engaged in the Battle of the Bulge, was trying to rescue the brave men of the 101st. Our minds and prayers were on the men at the front line who were freezing, fighting, and dying to save us all. We all talked about wanting to help, and it wasn't long before we got that chance.

It was mid-December when they mustered us all out on the tarmac at Molesworth. It was a gloomy, overcast day. The weather had been lousy for two weeks, and as a result, our B-17 Fortresses had not been able to fly any missions. Our commanding officer (CO) told us the men at Bastogne were still surrounded and freezing, and Patton's Third Army needed infantry soldiers. We all hoped to finish the war in the coming spring, but Hitler and the Wehrmacht had launched their winter attack and surprised us all. Our men were unprepared and poorly supplied. The Ardennes Offensive had revitalized the German army, and we were faced with the possibility of defeat once more.

Our CO told us he needed volunteers to gather their gear and fly to Belgium immediately. There, they would be assembled into relief companies and marched to the front. He repeated this was strictly a volunteer mission, and if anyone declined, it would not be held against them. I couldn't help but think about Doolittle Raiders, who were all volunteers. This kind of patriotism was everywhere in the war—men volunteering to put their lives at risk fighting for their country without a second thought. I have heard World War II referred to as the "Patriotic War," and I have to agree. Our freedom was in jeopardy, our country was unified, and we all knew the seriousness of the aggression in the souls of our enemies.

"All those wanting to volunteer, take one step forward, now," our CO said.

Without hesitation, nearly the entire squadron stepped forward simultaneously. I heard the brush of the men's uniforms and the sound of our boots contacting the tarmac in unison. The sound was deafening, and I remember feeling the ground shake. I definitely felt the air move. Then there were the stragglers—those who paused a moment longer than the others. They stepped forward next. In the end, only a handful of men did not accept the challenge. I don't know why, and I don't blame them. Maybe they had family members who needed them. No one said a thing about it.

It was a sight I will never forget. I think even the generals were taken aback by the number of men who answered the call. It was patriotism like no other. Starting at the end of our very long line, a group of officers began to count off the volunteers one by one. After each man gave his name and serial number, he peeled off from the formation, returned to the barracks, and packed his gear.

I stood at attention and listened as the group came nearer. I could feel the excitement and fear coursing through my veins. Then my heart sank. When the officers were only two men away from me, they announced they had filled their quota and no more volunteers were needed. I know I should have felt relieved, but I didn't. I was disappointed beyond words. I can't explain it other than I felt as if this were my opportunity to play a real part in the war, to go to battle, and if needed, die defending my country and the cause of liberty. I was also afraid this would be my *final* opportunity to do that.

As it turned out, I was right. I still have a hard time reconciling that day. I had always been at the front of the class because my name started with *A*. I hadn't always liked it, but I was used to being first. This time I was not first in line. I was near the end, and I wished more than anything I wasn't. The only way I can rationalize that event is through my faith in God. He has a plan for all of us, and I suppose his plan for me did not include fighting in the Battle of the Bulge. I did all I could and would have done whatever I was asked to do. I felt that way then, and I feel the same way now.

BATTLEFIELD OF POVERTY

I remember us all cheering when our troops were rescued at Bastogne. I say they were rescued, but I also acknowledge that *they* never felt they needed rescuing. From that point on, the war moved quickly. Before we knew it, Germany surrendered on May 9, 1945. We were joyous, but at the same time, our collective attention turned to the Pacific Theater, where our boys were still fighting the Empire of Japan. The men of the 303rd were sent to Morocco as relief. Our planes did not accompany us.

I don't remember much of our time there; it was not very interesting, and we were not there long. The two things I do remember were not pleasant. In Morocco, we did not lose men to the battlefield of freedom; we lost them to the battlefield of poverty. Casablanca was such a poor city. The officers told the enlisted men never to walk alone or go to the market area, called the Casbah.

"You will be killed for a stick of gum," they told us.

I don't think any of us believed it, but it was true. Soldiers would go down the market streets of the Casbah and never return. Our men were being killed for their shoes, their clothes, and believe it or not, their mattress covers. Murderers and thieves would cut a hole in the middle of the bed covers for their heads and wear them as robes. *That's insanity*, I thought. I had known extreme poverty, but I couldn't image killing anyone for any reason other than the one that took me to war: the defense of freedom and liberty.

The other unpleasant event in Morocco happened when I was in Tunisia, where we were deployed as a police force. General Charles de Gaulle came to the city of Tunis on a diplomatic mission. As part of the ceremony, we soldiers lined the streets of Tunis, unit by unit, and stood at attention in our dress uniforms. Standing at attention was just that—no movement, no talking, nothing. This was unpleasant but not unbearable. What *was* unbearable was the putrid smell coming from the ground. The stench was so bad I nearly gagged. When I glanced down, I saw brown water running at my feet. In that instant I realized the water trickling over my boots was raw sewage. We stood for over an hour as the dignitaries passed, holding back the urge to vomit. When we got back to the barracks, we scrubbed our boots so clean I think they changed colors.

North Africa was a holding place. It was like marking time, and I was more than pleased when we got our orders to depart. We were finally going back to the States, but we were not going back home. Douglas MacArthur and Admiral Nimitz had driven the Japanese out of the islands of the Pacific Rim and back to their homeland, but Japan was far from conquered. We were transported from the Tunis Port by C-47s to Mather Field near Sacramento, California, where we awaited our deployment to the Pacific Theater.

Mather Field was an aerial port of embarkation tasked with the mission of redeploying large numbers of men and aircraft from Europe. Some said we would lose 100,000 men while invading Japan, but that never happened. There were rumors going around the base that we had a surprise for Japan—a secret weapon. We heard many similar stories throughout the war, so I didn't pay much attention to this one. We were being issued new gear designed specifically for our fight against the Japanese, and I was focusing my mind and body on that. Everything we were issued for battle in Europe had to be turned in. After waging war for over three and a half years, our military had become extremely efficient at transporting and equipping troops.

Our military had also become extremely good at having troops stand in line. At times, I felt like we stood in line waiting to stand in line. We gathered the uniforms we were issued for Europe and stood in line to turn them in. We stood in line to receive our new uniforms for battle in Japan. It seemed like we did this for every piece of gear we had. It was a tedious and time-consuming process, but tedium is part of war.

After standing in lines for most of the day, I returned to the barracks before heading to the chow hall for supper. There were always new faces in the barracks, as soldiers were constantly shipped in and out. It was a seemingly endless line of men and equipment. As I reached my bunk, I heard a commotion and some angry words from the bunks next to mine. I heard something familiar in the raised voices—something from the past. I looked over and was surprised to see my dear family friend Woodrow Mansur. I couldn't believe it. In all this humanity, what were the chances of running into someone from Freeman Street?

The sight of such a familiar face sent me back to my old neighborhood. I remembered walking past Woody's house. It was rainy and cold. I had no coat. Mrs. Mansur saw me through her window and yelled for me to come inside. Of course, I did as I was told. She walked into Woody's room and brought out one of his coats.

"Here, Ralph. This is yours now," she said.

I started to argue, but she gave me a motherly stare and placed the coat on my shoulders. Woody never said a thing about it to me. He knew it would only embarrass me. I never forgot his mother's love and generosity. I wore that coat until it literally fell apart.

Woody was always so good-natured; it was hard to see him upset now.

"Woody!" I yelled. He looked over, and his face lit up. His anger seemed to subside for a moment at the shock of seeing me. He ran over, and we embraced. This was home.

"What is wrong?" I asked him.

Woodrow began to complain bitterly. He was visibly upset about having spent most of the war stationed on the West Coast. Now that the war was almost over, he was being shipped to the Pacific. Woodrow had volunteered like the rest of us and wanted to do more than just a stint in California.

We were not there, but on August 9, 1945, we dropped an atomic bomb on the city of Hiroshima, Japan. The destruction was overwhelming, yet the emperor of Japan did not surrender until another bomb was dropped on the city of Nagasaki two days later.

General MacArthur accepted unconditional surrender from the empire of Japan aboard the battleship *Missouri* on August 14, 1945. Hitler was dead. Japan had surrendered. THE WAR WAS OVER!

Ralph was the last serviceman released from Ellington Air Force Base in Houston at the end of WWII. It was a momentous occasion that made the *Houston Chronicle*.

It took only moments for the US government to realize it was time to disband our military forces. There was a huge amount of celebration, and at the same time we were all getting orders to return to our local bases for debriefing and discharge. The movement of soldiers was like mosquitoes on stagnant water. Massive. Trains pulled up to the station and soldiers would jam into the cars. There was no standing room. Soldiers were hanging out of the doors and windows. I think I even remember seeing a soldier on top of a train car. Everyone wanted to get home as fast as possible.

I was ordered to Ellington Air Force Base in Clear Lake, Texas, which is between Houston and Galveston. We went through an extensive debriefing, during which the army oriented us to civilian life and reviewed the benefits we would receive as veterans. I was in the barracks early one morning when my CO called me to attention and ordered me to get dressed in my Class A uniform. I was to be the last man discharged from Ellington Field, and the army wanted to make it a media event. The *Houston Chronicle* was there to cover the story, and I made the front page. This was not exactly how I wanted to be depicted for my army service, but it brought pride to my family.

TEXAS CITY

I only celebrated my homecoming for a day or so before looking for work. The war was over, and it was time to get on with my life. I was struck by how much everything had changed and how much I had changed, too. When Johnnie and I left for the war, the country was just beginning to show signs of recovery. The economy had been improving as a result of building a war machine to defeat the Axis powers.

What I saw now was different. There was optimism in the air and opportunity was everywhere. I had to change my thinking. In the prewar years, I had sold apples, flowers, papers, and anything else I could to make a few pennies. After being exposed to at least part of the world, I wanted more for both myself and my family.

As a first step, I renewed my relationship with Mr. Hightower at Houston Title Company. I liked the title business and knew something about it. I also felt the owner was an honest person I could trust (that would change in time). Before the war I had been a courier—really nothing more than a delivery boy—but not now. With all the new housing construction, Houston Title needed to build a "plant," and Mr. Hightower turned to me.

If the three most important rules of real estate are location, location, location, the three most important rules of the title business are records, records, records. In the title business, building a "plant" means spending hours transcribing property information at the county office. It's a painstaking process, but once you have the records, your company is in the best position to do the title work. At Houston Title we focused our business on lots in the eastern part of town. We thought that part of Houston would grow, and we were right. I spent the next year building the "plant" for Houston Title and had between six and eight people working for me.

The work was tedious, but I knew it would pay dividends, so I made sure we kept our noses to the grindstone. At the same time, I learned about the GI Bill, which offered returning soldiers the option of higher education. For the first time in my life, I had a chance to get a college education. No one in my family had gone to college, so I seized the opportunity as soon as I could. There is no better way to improve your lot in life than with education. I enrolled at the University of Houston for the spring semester of 1946. Johnnie didn't get home from the navy until May of that year. By that time, I already had a semester under my belt.

It had been over three years since I had seen or spoken to my brother. We communicated through Mom or V-mail—no, not e-mail, V-mail, also known as Victory Mail. In V-mail, soldiers wrote messages and sergeants read them for sensitive information. Then messages were transferred to microfilm to reduce weight before being shipped overseas. After shipping, messages were reproduced at about half the size and delivered to the addressee.

Johnnie, Juliette, Libbie (their mother), and Ralph (in his late twenties) in Houston, Texas, soon after both Ralph and Johnnie returned home from WWII.

Louis, Juliette, Johnnie, standing on the car running board; Libbie (mother) and Tolfie (father), standing middle row; Jack (left) and George (right), kneeling; about the time when Ralph and Johnnie returned from WWII.

You could only write on one side of the paper, and you were limited to a few sentences. It was difficult to say much on a tiny piece of paper. Usually, my messages looked something like: *Hello, How are you? Don't worry, I am doing fine! Love Ralph.* Johnnie would send back much the same, so we really only knew we were both alive, nothing more.

I remember the day Johnnie came home from the navy. He was still dressed in his crisp white uniform. To his disappointment, he arrived at an empty house. It wasn't long before we all started trickling home, and there, sitting on the front porch swing, was Johnnie. He looked so manly and grown up waiting for us with his bell-bottoms swaying in the breeze. The song "Bell Bottom Trousers" was popular on the radio back then. I wondered how many girls were waiting for him.

One by one we walked up to the house. Seeing Johnnie sitting there was almost like seeing a ghost. We knew it was him, but we couldn't believe it. Mom was the final one to arrive. As she walked closer to the house, you could see her eyebrows squint together and make a puzzled look on her face. She froze.

"Mom, it's me! I'm home!" Johnnie yelled out.

In an instant Mom flew to the porch and he leapt out of the swing. Tears rolled down both of their faces as they embraced. Mom cried and thanked God for sending her son home. Now all her children were home and safe.

The war had changed Johnnie, just as it had changed me. You cannot go through a world war and not be transformed. Johnnie had also filled out even more than I had. He was bigger now, but the distinctive curl on his forehead remained, as it would the rest of his life.

After spending a few months with me at Houston Title, Johnnie enrolled at the University of Texas (UT) in the fall of 1946. He moved to Elgin—only thirty miles from Austin and UT—to live with our grandmother, Sadie. After the navy, Johnnie thought it was best to venture out and live in a different city, and Grandmother's house was free. Medicine intrigued him, and he thought the family could use a doctor. But despite his best efforts, becoming a doctor was not meant to be. Johnnie could not pass Chemistry 101. The periodic table was a mystery to him. When the spring semester of 1947 rolled around, he decided to come home and try something different. We talked endlessly about his options and my excitement about law school. I convinced Johnnie to join me.

I worked at Houston Title during the day and attended school at night and on Saturdays. Johnnie and George worked at the Southern Pacific Railroad and also joined me at school. We were lucky the University of Houston offered so many evening classes. I remember my friends asking me how we could work all day and go to school at night.

"Easy. We could never just stay at home. It's not in our nature," I replied.

If I hadn't been going to school at night, I would have taken a second job. It was just inconceivable to have that much free time and not do something productive with it. When I was a child, working was a matter of survival; now, it had become a habit.

I have to admit the rewards of working and making a good living outweighed the satisfaction of getting an education, even though I knew education was more important. It's not that I didn't like school, but it was so theoretical it just didn't seem real to me. Houston Title seemed real. Everything we did had a purpose and an objective. There was no wasted effort, and the goal was always clear.

Houston Title was accommodating when it came to school. I took as many night courses as I could, but not everything was offered at night, which meant I had to go to school during the day sometimes. I tried to cram all my day courses in on Wednesday mornings. One Wednesday, I found myself involved in one of the worst industrial accidents in US history.

I walked out of class for a short break. April 16, 1947, was a beautiful day—the sky was blue, and the humidity of summer had not yet settled in. I was thinking about what I had to do at work that afternoon when I heard a massive explosion. It wasn't long before I felt it too. I heard my share of explosions in the war, but this was bigger than anything I had ever heard.

All of us standing outside looked at each other in surprise and wonderment. Then someone—I don't remember who—pointed to the south.

"Look!" they yelled.

There, silhouetted against the spring sky, was a growing mushroom-shaped cloud. My first thought was of the attack on Pearl Harbor and then our attack on the Japanese at Hiroshima and Nagasaki. Had some other country attacked us again, only this time with a nuclear weapon? After all, the Houston Ship Channel was one of the largest ports in the world.

In those days, our best source of information was the radio. After quickly looking around to see what others were doing, I ran to my 1938 Buick, put my keys in the ignition, and switched on the radio. It only took a few minutes before a newsman broke into the local program and announced the emergency.

"An explosion at a dock in Texas City has left many dead and the city stunned. Volunteers are needed!"

That was all I had to hear. It didn't matter what had to be done. I knew I had to help.

I rushed to a pay phone and called my brother.

"Johnnie!" I must have screamed into the phone. "There has been a terrible disaster at the docks in Texas City. They need help!"

"I'm in! Are you on your way to get me?" Johnnie yelled back.

"Yes, I'll be there in twenty minutes. Be ready and get Dad!"

I'm sure my voice was at maximum volume by then.

When I got to the house, Johnnie and Dad were waiting on the front porch. Volunteers were to meet at Houston City Hall, so that is where we headed. Cars and people surrounded City Hall. Police officers directed us toward the Red Cross truck, which had pulled up only moments earlier. We did as we were instructed. My car stopped with a squeak of the brakes, and we all jumped out. I'm not sure if the people from the Red Cross knew exactly what to do at this point, so they asked for a volunteer to be the lead car. My hand shot up before I could even think.

"We'll do it!" I heard myself yell.

The officer in charge pointed to me.

"Son, pull up to the corner. You will be the lead car! Fill it up with medical supplies—all you can take!" he said.

They filled every square inch of our old '38 Buick with bandages and medications. I remember looking in the back and seeing rolls of gauze and surgical tape filling the seat beside my father. There was so much going on. People were lining up behind us and filling their cars with whatever the Red Cross gave them. In an instant, we were on the road to Texas City.

Johnnie, Dad, and I were leading the way. I was anxious but excited. I could feel the butterflies in my stomach. I looked at Johnnie and smiled. He smiled back. We spent the war in different branches of the service and half a world apart, but not now. This was our chance to do something together. I spied my father in the rearview mirror and noticed he had an odd little smirk on his face. He never said it, but I think the smirk came from watching the two of us—his two oldest boys. I knew he was proud of us.

I pressed the accelerator to the floor of that old Buick, but it wouldn't go any faster. I looked in the rearview mirror and saw the line of cars stacked up behind us. I jammed my foot down even harder, but nothing changed. We were going as fast as we were going to go. The people behind me never honked their horns, though they must have wanted to.

I was really starting to worry about our pace when Johnnie yelled from the passenger seat.

"Ralph, look! Police cars are coming right at us! What's going on?"

I looked toward the oncoming lane and saw the police cars. Their sirens were blasting.

"Stop your cars! Pull over! There's going to be another explosion!" a voice blared over the loudspeaker.

I jerked the car to the right and slammed on the brakes. I can still see Johnnie, Dad, and me jumping out of the car and throwing ourselves in a ditch. We lay there with Dad between Johnnie and me. I felt Dad's hand covering my head and saw his other hand was on top of Johnnie's. This was the first time I remember feeling like he was protecting us. Even at twenty-three years old, it was a comfort. I never knew how much I missed it until that moment.

It wasn't long before the police called us out of the ditch.

"Back to your cars!" they shouted. "We're in the clear for now."

We didn't know how long we were in the clear, but we did know there were people who needed our help. Without hesitation, we jumped back into the car, fired up the engine, and headed toward the thick column of black smoke.

As we approached the dock area, I couldn't believe my eyes. The devastation was beyond belief. I could see Johnnie was equally stunned. Dad was speechless for a long while. Then I heard him say, "God have mercy on these people. Boys, let's see what we can do to help."

Every single structure at the dock was affected in some way. Many were completely knocked down by the blast or burned by the fires. Others just had their windows blown out. There were people wandering all over the streets. Most seemed to be in a daze, as if they were trying to reconcile what happened. I couldn't help but think all these people went to work that morning expecting a day just like any other. None of them had expected this. How could they?

We made our way to the aid station and unloaded our supplies. The cars behind us were directed to other aid stations set up around the city. We looked for what else we could do to help. My father's directions still rang fresh in my ears. It wasn't hard to see the people wandering the streets needed help. We approached them one by one and escorted them to the triage stations.

"What happened?" most of them said.

We heard that a ship filled with fertilizer caught fire and then exploded. No one could believe it.

When we reached the triage station, the nurses sat the victims down and assessed their injuries. I remembered doing much of the same when we pulled our brave men from the bellies of the B-17s at Molesworth. It was always easy to assess the external injuries—cuts and broken bones. It was harder to determine the extent of internal injuries. A person could look practically normal but could then fall down dead from internal bleeding within twenty minutes. This scared me the most; I'm sure it scared the nurses too. How do you decide who gets treatment immediately and who waits? This split-second decision often means life or death.

After we finished with triage, we were asked to help with the corpses. Hours after the initial explosion, there were still unretrieved dead bodies. The closer we got to the dock and the flaming ship, the more bodies we saw. We didn't know it at the time, but one of the reasons the Texas City explosion was so devastating was because the fire trucks were set up too close to the ship. When the fertilizer exploded, the blast destroyed the trucks and killed the firefighting crews. This snuffed out the city's ability to fight the blaze, which then marauded through the town, unabated.

I saw some horrific sights during my time at Molesworth Field, but I never saw anything like this. The sight of charred humans assaulted my eyes, and I could hardly hold back the impulse to retch at the smell of singed flesh. Dad, Johnnie, and I stood around our first dead body and looked aghast. No one said a word. We all knew we had a job to do, and we needed to get to it. I bent down and grabbed the wrists as Johnnie grabbed the ankles. Dad stood near the middle of the body and prepared to lift the bulk of the weight.

As I lifted, I felt my grip fail. I squeezed harder, but it did no good. The wrists slipped out of my hands. I looked down and saw my hands held nothing but charred skin. I looked up in horror and saw the same had happened to Johnnie at the ankles. Johnnie and I took off our shirts, tore them in half, and wrapped them around our hands. We got our grip again, with better results this time. As Johnnie and I lifted the body, Dad moved in and grasped the waist. I'm not sure how he held the weight, but he did. We made our way to the makeshift morgue and laid the body next to the others. We repeated this process many times, but we never got used to it.

It was getting late in the day. I don't know how many bodies we retrieved. I didn't want to count. Johnnie and Dad had gone for water, and I stood staring through the broken windows of the building that was now the morgue. Dead bodies were stacked six high, some with clothes still on and some without. Some were mangled beyond recognition, others completely intact. The gruesome scene still plays in my head and sends chills down my spine, even today.

We worked side by side until late in the evening. When the relief crews saw we could not walk another step, they sent us home. I was so tired I didn't know if I could drive, so Dad did while Johnnie and I slept. Before I closed my eyes, I watched my father as he sat behind the wheel. He had strength like no other.

Dad was a bit of a mystery to us. Our relationship was distant. Johnnie and I judged him for not being around when we were growing up and struggling to survive. But that day at the dock, I looked at him through a new pair of eyes. I could see my father as a man who had talents and frailties just like the rest of us.

When you are young and poor, it's hard to watch your father walk out the door in the evening and not return until well after you've gone to bed, or sometimes for days. A child cannot know what goes through a man's heart. But as a man, I began to understand he did the best he could for his family.

HE WAS UNREMARKABLE EXCEPT FOR HIS MIND

Despite the devastation in Texas City, Houston continued to boom and so did our family. My dear mother still baked bread early every morning, and my younger brothers continued the legacy of selling flowers in the spring, newspapers after school, and apples on Saturdays at the department store. With Johnnie and me at the title company during the day and everyone else working jobs, our family was bringing in more money than ever before. As a result, our spirits and expectations began to grow.

Because of my work ethic while building the title plant and helping grow the business, I was promised an executive position leading to partnership. Once the plant was complete, I began doing marketing for the company and I brought in commercial clients. Business was booming and all I could think about was my future.

During this time, I met a remarkable man who changed my life. While I was marketing to commercial realtors, I came across a seventy-five-year-old man who, for some reason, took a liking to me. He might have been impressed by my tenacity, or perhaps he saw a little of himself in me because I was ambitious and willing to work hard. Whatever the reason, Mr. George Washington Nesmith took me under his wing and taught me how to use the knowledge I had gained in the title business to buy and develop properties of my own. It was my first step toward getting off the treadmill of working for others.

Our relationship started with a knock on the door of a tiny wood-framed building. It was an unremarkable-looking structure, and George Nesmith was an unremarkable-looking man. When I met him, his hair was white and virtually everything about him was average—height, weight, build—except his mind. George had a keen sense for business and real estate. He taught me how to identify and assess property and how to put a deal together. Most people were unimpressed by George because of his small office, lack of a secretary, and unimposing looks, but they were the ones who missed out. I learned not to judge a book by its cover—for if you do, you truly miss out. I learned this lesson early in my career, and it served me well my entire life.

I had regular contact with George in those days. I supplied him with property information such as legal descriptions and ownership, and he always found the time to help me with my ideas. It was with George's assistance and guidance that I acquired and developed my first property—a lot at the east end of town on Long Drive. I studied it for what seemed like forever and then went to George with my plan. He said it had merit, and so I moved forward.

I acquired the property with a loan from the bank, and a few months later I had an interested tenant. George helped me market the property to a man who wanted to manufacture small boats. I had a fabricated metal building installed, and my first tenant moved in. I remember the excitement and relief of getting the lease agreement signed—excitement for having closed the deal and relief that I would be able to pay the banknote. I relived this feeling with every real estate deal. And with every deal I made, I always thought of my friend George Washington Nesmith.

MY DEAR ADELENE

Before I knew it, I was twenty-nine years old, in my last year of law school and for the first time in my life seriously considering a family of my own. As with nearly everything else in my life, my family had a part in this as well. Many years earlier, Uncle George, Mom's brother, worked for a man named John Shawhean at Blue Bonnet, the margarine company. Mr. Shawhean was from Fort Worth and was also Lebanese. During one Sunday dinner at my grandmother's house, Uncle George mentioned Mr. Shawhean's beautiful daughter would be in Galveston the next week.

"Ralph, would you be interested in showing her around?" he asked.

"Sure. Of course—why not?" I said, though I knew nothing about Galveston Island.

Uncle George immediately went to the phone, called Mr. Shawhean, and gave him the news. I remember hearing my uncle's conversation.

"A picture? A picture of Ralph? Okay, I'll find one and send it," he said.

I was taken aback.

"Who wants a picture of me, Uncle?" I asked.

He looked down at his shoes for a moment.

"Mr. Shawhean's daughter, Adelene, wants to see what you look like before committing to go out with you," he stuttered.

I felt the anger start in my toes; my voice began to rise.

"A picture of me!? I am doing her a favor, and she wants a picture of me?"

My uncle calmed me down. He told me I was actually doing *him* the favor and asked me to please get a picture to send to Fort Worth, so I did as my uncle requested. I guess I was approved because the next week Uncle George and I were off to Galveston. I was told to behave myself because she was a good girl from a good family. *Of course I'll behave myself*! I thought. *Who does Uncle George think I am?*

We arrived in Galveston and awaited the train from Fort Worth. The train pulled in on time and we saw a mass of people exiting the cars, porters moving bags, and people appearing and disappearing among the plumes of steam. I was struck by one passenger in particular. Out of the corner of my eye I spied a classy, beautiful, dark-haired woman dressed in a stylish suit and hat. She was giving orders to the bellhops, pointing to this suitcase and that one, ordering them to pick them up and follow her as if she were royalty.

I wondered who this woman was. Part of me was intimidated. I had seen many people give orders to others and sometimes to me. Another part of me was completely intrigued. The way she moved with flowing grace. The way her confidence was unwavering. And her beauty was simply stunning.

The beautiful Adelene, at the time Ralph met her.

I took a break from my trance to scan the crowd for the woman I had come to meet. I leaned over to my uncle.

"Well, where is this special woman, Uncle George? Do you think she changed her mind after receiving my photo?" I asked sarcastically.

"No, son. Here she is," he replied, pointing to the woman who had left me starstruck.

I stood with my mouth open for a second. When I regained my composure, I was thrilled. Deep inside I had been praying she was the one. I walked up to her confidently and introduced myself. She looked me over.

"You are much better looking in person," she said.

We left the train station for the plush Hotel Galvez. Adelene had brought her best friend Gloria. They settled into their room while Uncle George and I went to ours. I was intoxicated by Adelene's beauty and charm. I knew I had found the love of my life, but I was from meager beginnings, and she was obviously from a family of means. How could we bridge the gap? Later on, I would find it comforting that she didn't seem to see the obstacles that I saw—but I would learn her father did.

That night we all went out to dinner. Uncle George and I met Adelene and Gloria in the lobby of the Hotel Galvez. My uncle drove; the girls and I sat in the back. I'm not sure how it happened, but I ended up sitting between them. The evening was charged with electricity, and I found myself taking turns stealing kisses from Adelene and then Gloria. They were only pecks on the cheek. The girls objected but giggled just the same.

My uncle's objections were more serious. He looked in the rearview mirror and reminded me these were good girls, and

I should be more respectful. I'm sure it also occurred to him that Adelene was the daughter of his former boss. I remember nodding my head and then kissing the girls again. The third time this happened, my uncle looked in the mirror again, more sternly than before.

"*Abushoon!*" he said, which is Arabic for "Shame on you!"

I'd never learned to speak Arabic fluently, but I knew what this meant. I always respected family. It was time for me to stop playing around.

Johnnie and I double-dated often, and I had arranged for him to come down and meet Gloria. When I told him Adelene brought her best friend, he came in a flash, no questions asked, no pictures needed. Johnnie met us at the restaurant, and the girls went crazy for him. I was not surprised when he and Gloria hit it off.

We danced and laughed the night away. I remember being so sure of my feelings for Adelene that I asked her how many children she wanted.

"Four!" she replied without hesitation.

Perfect, I thought, *just the right number*. I fell even more in love with her on the dance floor. I loved to dance, and she did too. We made a great pair. Later, people called us the Fred Astaire and Ginger Rogers of the Lebanese community.

At the end of the evening, Johnnie and I took the girls back to their hotel room. The next day, however, something a bit embarrassing happened. I dropped Johnnie and Gloria off at the seawall while Adelene and I sat in the car. We talked and talked and, okay, we also kissed a little. It was a hot August day and the car windows fogged up. When Johnnie and Gloria returned, they knocked on the window ever so gently, as if they were interrupting something. They weren't, but I never could convince them otherwise.

Parting Saturday at midnight, we decided to finish the weekend in Houston. We met the very next evening. Johnnie and I drove from Galveston to our home in North Houston, forty-five miles away. Uncle George stayed on the island. Adelene and Gloria took the short flight from Galveston to Houston and then taxied to the Rice Hotel.

We spent the next evening together, starting with dinner at the Rice Hotel and then dancing. Things were moving fast for me. I met this woman only a day earlier, but I felt as if I had known her all my life. I found time to date regularly despite work and school since returning from the war—a testament to a young man's ingenuity and energy—but in all that time, I never met anyone like my dear Adelene. She simply made my head spin.

My life was moving fast in other ways, too. Only a day before meeting this divine creature from Fort Worth, I received notification that I had passed the State Bar of Texas, the culmination of years of school and study. And to top it off, I passed the first time, which only twenty percent of those who take it can say.

I can't tell you how relieved and excited I was; I finally felt my hard work, tenacity, and belief in God and myself were paying off. Uncle William, the man who showed me how to make money by selling apples and papers, always told me the importance of a positive attitude.

"I don't care what happened yesterday, good or bad; ya gotta put your boots on every morning and make something of yourself," he would say.

At ten years old, I don't think I really knew what he meant.

In those days, I didn't even have a pair of boots, not to mention shoes. Still, I never forgot what Uncle William said and I did my best to live it every day of my life. Even today, I know I still have to put my boots on and make something of myself.

Adelene left for Fort Worth on Monday morning. Before she boarded her flight, she called to thank me for a lovely time. Though I had a wonderful time too, something inside me told me to hold back. Despite my feelings, I didn't want to gush or sound too smitten.

"Ralph, I don't know where this relationship is going—," she began.

Words flew out of my mouth before I could stop them.

"Relationship?" I interjected. "I am a confirmed bachelor."

There was silence on the phone.

"Oh," she said flatly.

I felt as if the air had left both our lungs. Neither of us could speak.

To this day I am not sure why I said that. I suppose it could have been an involuntary reaction, like when the doctor hits someone's knee with one of those oddly shaped hammers. After all, I had told several women of my confirmed bachelor status. Or perhaps it was instinctual. Like a mustang being corralled, my first impulse was to bolt. But regardless of the reason, this was the first time in my life I didn't mean what I said. I knew I was falling in love with Adelene, and I had to see her again.

Every weekend from that day forward, I drove to Fort Worth to see Adelene. I would leave after work on Friday and make record time on the two-lane highway. All I could think of was Adelene. I took many stupid chances—driving too fast, passing

18-wheelers on a dark, winding road—but it was all worth it. I'd arrive late on Friday night and considered it a good trip if I pulled into my motel before midnight.

We dated for six months, which meant six months of me driving to Fort Worth every weekend. Adelene's mother, Altus, was a gracious and kind woman. She always welcomed me into their home with open arms. Strangely, I never met Adelene's father until much later. Every time I went to her house he would be gone, mysteriously, either hunting or fishing. There was always some excuse. I politely asked to meet him several times, but there was never an answer, just a look of uncertainty from Adelene.

Even though Adelene was half Lebanese, she did not know much about our culture; nor had she dated anyone who was Lebanese.

"My grandmother prayed daily that I would marry a good Lebanese man," she told me one evening. Supposedly her dad didn't care either way, but I was not getting that feeling at all. I thought he did care, but he certainly didn't care for me.

I was getting the same bad feeling at work. I began to question my future at Houston Title. I had worked for them before the war as a courier, and after the war I had built the title plant—which meant I'd built their business. But despite my hard work and their promises, I was being passed over for promotion after promotion. The owner was advancing his family members over me. I spoke with him and he assured me the next promotion—president of the North Houston branch—would be mine. A month later the position was awarded to another family member.

I knew I had to move on. There was no future for me in the company. After the litany of broken promises, I suppose I should have been angry, but I wasn't. There was no point in it. I'd seen too many people become consumed by what could have been. It simply was what it was, and I learned sometimes God closes a door for a reason.

After looking around for a short period of time, I found a promising position at Mainland Mortgage. I was gratified to find it paid more than what I was making at Houston Title and also had more potential for advancement. I had just passed the bar and the world was, once again, a bright and wondrous place.

Around this time, I found myself sitting in a closing for a residential property in the Oak Forest subdivision. It was an all brick, two-bedroom single story that most people considered a starter home. I told myself all along I was purchasing this home as an investment property, but a voice inside my head told me there was another reason.

Only a few days after the closing I found out what the other reason was. I called Adelene in the middle of the week, which was unusual. I couldn't wait until the weekend to tell her the news. We exchanged hellos, and I got straight to the point.

"Adelene, I bought a house a few days ago," I said.

There was a pause.

"Why did you do that, Ralph?" she asked.

The words flowed.

"For us!" I said. "We'll need a place to live."

"A place for *us* to live?" she questioned.

"Yes!" I replied.

"Is this a proposal, Ralph?" Adelene exclaimed excitedly.

"Yes, it is."

It was almost as if I were hearing someone else speak the words, but there was no one else around. I felt the tension grow inside me. I realized I had placed this call for no other purpose than to propose to my love. Now I was waiting for her answer. I don't know how much time actually passed, but it felt like forever. Then I heard her speak the words that would forever make me happy.

"Well, then, I accept."

I called Mrs. Shawhean the very same day to tell her of my desire for Adelene's hand in marriage. I am sure that she already knew, but she didn't let on; she allowed me the grace of telling her in my own way.

"Mrs. Shawhean, I would like to arrange a time to meet Adelene's father. I have been driving to Fort Worth for the past six months and have yet to see him. I thought you might help me with the arrangements," I said.

"Ralph, why you don't come to the house this Saturday around noon?" she replied in her sweet, calm voice. "Bring your family. You will need them. I think they will help your cause. By the way, Mr. Shawhean likes a good cigar or an aged bourbon. Why don't you bring one as a gift?"

The following Friday, Mom, Dad, Aunt Lula, Uncle George, his wife, Mabel, and I drove to Fort Worth for the Saturday high noon showdown. I decided to get a good bottle of bourbon as my offering. I think I was more nervous that day than I was the night I shipped out to England for the war.

We arrived at the house on time. Mrs. Shawhean answered the door and gracefully let us all in. She led us into the living room. There, sitting in a big, overstuffed chair, was John Shawhean. He was larger than life with a cigar firmly planted between his teeth while he glared at me like I was Lucifer himself. He wore a tan three-piece suit and a pocket watch hung from his vest—the only thing missing was a hat.

Uncle George took the lead and broke the ice. I don't remember what he said, I only know how incredibly relieved I was that the awkward silence was broken. I think it was a full five minutes before Mr. Shawhean invited us to sit. Again, there was silence, and again, Uncle George broke the stalemate with conversation. My mother and Aunt Lula stood on either side of me the whole time and never said a word. Oddly enough, Mr. Shawhean never talked to them either. He simply acknowledged their presence upon the initial introduction and that was it.

When my uncle finally ran out of pleasantries, the conversation fell to me. Adelene's father knew why I was there, but he was not going to make it easy. In fact, I'm sure it was a test. If he could keep me from asking for his daughter's hand in marriage, I certainly was not the man for her.

He looked at me dead-on.

"Ralph," he said in his deep, gruff voice, "follow me."

I was not sure if I was about to be executed or brought into the family. He led me out to the veranda. The door closed behind us and he stood in front of me.

I approached Adelene's father as I had been taught to approach the bench—with reverence, but also with a purpose. I strode to within a pace or two of Mr. Shawhean. He held his ground.

"Mr. Shawhean, I am in love with your daughter, Mary Adelene. I've come to ask you for her hand in marriage."

There was silence. And then there was more silence.

I decided to take a different tack.

"I would like your blessing for our marriage," I announced. My voice was firm; it did not waver or crack. But he stood there as if it had. At first, he continued to stare at me. The cigar firmly clinched between his teeth. After what seemed like an eon, I heard his gruff voice.

"Why don't we sit?"

As we moved to the chairs, he sized me up as a boxer might size up a sparring partner. I'm sure if he wanted to, he could have knocked me down with a single blow, but he didn't. We sat in opposing chairs and after he settle in, he said abruptly, "Let me see the ring."

I took this as a good sign. At least he was considering the proposal. Or so I thought.

I dug in the pocket of my coat for a second or two and produced a small jewelry box. I stood, took a giant step forward, and offered the ring to the huge man sitting in the chair, scowling at me.

"Here it is, Mr. Shawhean."

I held the ring box before him, and he paused for an awkward moment, all the time glaring into my eyes. He took the box, brought it up near his face, and slowly pried it open. The hinges creaked. I watched his reaction as he caught sight of the diamond I was so proud of. With his enormous fingers he plucked the ring from its velvet resting place and held it up to the light. He examined it as if he were a jeweler trying to determine if it was real or fake. I'm sure he was trying to do the same with me.

I glanced through the glass panes of the veranda doors, where I spied the heads of my mother, Aunt Lula, Uncle George, and Adelene's mother, Altus, all staring at me. Uncle George was waving his arms and pointing toward my feet. I quickly realized what he was doing. I looked down. There sat the gift I had planned to give the irascible Mr. Shawhean.

Adelene's father finally lowered the ring and gave me a long stare.

"Not bad for the first one," he said.

I was elated. I was not going to let a window of opportunity pass. There was no better time to offer him my gift.

"Mr. Shawhean, I understand you appreciate fine bourbon from time to time. I brought you this."

Again, I stood, offered him the package, and returned to my seat. As he opened the carefully wrapped package, I snuck a peek back through the doors. My mother was smiling, as was Aunt Lula. Uncle George was giving me a thumbs up. Adelene's mother still looked concerned.

As Mr. Shawhean pulled the bottle of well-aged bourbon, the corners of his mouth turned up ever so slightly. It was there and gone in an instant. Then he looked at me sternly as he sat slightly forward in his chair.

"What is it that you do, anyway?" he asked.

I sat up in my chair.

"I currently work for a mortgage company, but I have recently passed the Texas State Bar exam and plan to practice law," I responded.

He looked at me sideways for a moment. I was not sure if he thought I was lying or if he just didn't like lawyers.

"Well, how much do you make?" he asked.

"I make almost three hundred a month," I announced proudly.

Mr. Shawhean sat back in his chair and removed the well-chewed cigar from his teeth.

"Three hundred a month? Son, do you realize that my daughter was born with a silver spoon in her mouth?"

I didn't know how to respond. Both yes and no seemed fraught with danger. If I said yes, he would think I was presumptuous. If I said no, he would think I wasn't paying attention. As it turned out, I didn't have to answer at all, as he asked a second question before I could answer the first.

"Do you really think you can take care of her in the manner to which she is accustomed?"

I knew the answer to this question and offered it without hesitation.

"Yes, I think I can, sir."

He looked at me with an almost comical expression as if to say, *You think you can, but you really don't know, do you, son?*

Mr. Shawhean motioned to the group staring through the windowpanes to open the door. Mrs. Shawhean did as her husband requested.

"Please ask Mary Adelene to come out," he commanded.

It wasn't long before Adelene appeared in the doorway. My heart melted.

"Adelene," he said, "is this what you want?"

"Yes," she replied.

He asked her again, this time a bit more sternly.

"Are you sure, honey? Is this man who you want?"

She looked him right in the eye, walked over, and gave him a kiss on the cheek.

"Yes, Daddy, this is who I want to marry."

The giant of a man softened. At that moment, I understood all he wanted was the best for his daughter.

A celebration ahead of Ralph and Adelene's marriage in 1952.
Seated from left to right are John Shawhean, Adelene's father; Mabel and
George Faour (George is Ralph's uncle, and he introduced him to Adelene);
Altus, Adelene's mother; Ralph and Adelene; and several family friends.

"Fine, then it shall be," he replied.

With that remark, the entire family came out to the veranda, everyone kissing, hugging, and celebrating. Mr. Shawhean even opened the bottle of bourbon I gave him, and we all toasted together.

FINGER SANDWICHES AND CAKE?

Within three months, we were married. The wedding was in Fort Worth, of course. I remember standing in the wings and waiting for the ceremony to begin. I didn't want to peek out and see who was in the pews, so I asked Johnnie, my best man, to do it for me. Johnnie looked out and began to laugh.

"What's wrong?" I asked.

"Nothing," Johnnie replied. "I just never realized the difference in our families."

"What *does* that mean?" I asked.

"Well, brother, on the bride's side of the church, they are already seated, with hands politely folded. Everyone's looking forward, and no one is talking. Our side . . . well, it is completely different. No one is sitting down. They are still filing in, talking, kissing, and hugging, and no one is looking forward."

Adelene's mother originally planned a small reception with punch, finger sandwiches, and cake. It hadn't been my place to comment on this, but my mother had no such restrictions. Libbie was typically shy and demure, but not when it came to this occasion. I don't know what she said to my soon-to-be in-laws, but it was made clear a Lebanese wedding reception included much more than finger sandwiches, mixed nuts, and cake.

My mother offered to go to Fort Worth and help with the cooking, but, to Mrs. Shawhean's credit, she declined. Altus was gracious enough to accept my mother's suggestions without reservation. Altus began to roll grape leaves and prepare the other food weeks ahead of time. She must have rolled grape leaves until her fingers were green. She froze everything in preparation for our feast.

I asked a very special Orthodox priest, Father Nahas, to officiate. He knew me and my family well. He was one of the traveling priests who visited our neighborhood. Father Nahas agreed, but on the Saturday before the wedding, there was a huge snowstorm in Nebraska, where he lived. The afternoon before the wedding, Father Nahas called to inform me he would not be able to make it. All flights were grounded. He was very upset, and so was I.

I understood, of course, but what was I going to do? Suddenly there was no priest, and the wedding was the next day. We were committed and the out-of-towners were already in Fort Worth. Everything was paid for and ready to go. The only thing missing was the person to marry us. It couldn't be just anybody; it had to be an Orthodox priest. There were not many in those days, and there was definitely not one in each city.

I heard there was a visiting priest in Austin, Father Rottle. I called him immediately. I told him of my predicament, but he had commitments of his own.

John Shawhean, looking "thrilled" to give his daughter, Adelene, away in marriage to Ralph. Adelene and Ralph married in Houston, Texas, in 1952.

Ralph and Adelene, known as the Fred Astaire and Ginger Rogers of the Lebanese community, fell in love on the dance floor. Here, they are dancing at their wedding.

"Ralph," he said, "I have a service to perform at 10 a.m. What time is your wedding?"

Our wedding wasn't until 5:30 in the afternoon. I felt a moment of relief, but once I began to calculate the timing, I realized it was going to be very close. Father Rottle would not finish the service in Austin until noon. He would have to travel from Austin to Fort Worth, and he didn't have a car. I made arrangements for him to take the 1 p.m. bus. This would get him in at 4:30 p.m., an hour before our service. I prayed there would not be any delays along the way.

Father Rottle got on the bus as scheduled. Johnnie picked him up at the station, and he arrived at the church at 5:20 p.m., a scant ten minutes early. I think I bit my nails to the nub, but it all worked out. The priest showed up, Adelene's father reluctantly walked her down the aisle, and I married the woman of my dreams.

The reception was everything Adelene and I hoped for. Our families got along famously. There was more delicious food than you could imagine—just as it should have been. John Shawhean and Adelene took the first dance, then my lovely bride and I kicked off our marriage by dancing to "Blue Tango."

We had never danced a tango before, but it was as if we had practiced for months. I was even amazed at how Adelene followed my lead as we glided across the dance floor. Many of Adelene's friends asked if I was a dance instructor. I appreciated the comment, but the truth was I just loved to dance, and I particularly loved to dance with my bride.

Looking back, there are only two things I regret about our wedding. One, I could only get three days off from work. I had just started with Mainland Mortgage and could only convince them to allow me three days. As a result, Adelene and I had to postpone our honeymoon until summer. Two, in all the confusion and excitement of the wedding preparation, I neglected to purchase a bed for our new house on Lamonte Street.

After spending our wedding night at the Adolphus Hotel in Dallas, Adelene and I arrived at our home to find my father, Johnnie, and Louis feverishly working to assemble the wedding present they had purchased for us. I was relieved they had taken care of something so important that I had neglected. I was shocked, however, when Adelene and I entered our bedroom to find not one, but two beds.

"Twin beds?!" I blurted out. I have to admit, I thought it was a joke at first.

Johnnie quickly took me aside.

"Brother, we were going to buy you a double bed, but these were on sale," he said.

Old habits die hard. We never paid full price for anything back then. I still don't. I was grateful, and I acknowledged their heartfelt attempt to make sure we had what we needed. Adelene and I still have those twin beds.

FROM BEHIND THE PILLAR SHE CAME

I was at Mainland Mortgage, and Adelene worked at South Western Drug as the assistant to the president. We enjoyed our friends and neighbors. Our weekends were filled with family, friends, fun, laughter, and playing cards. During the week, work was our focus. Life was great; I never knew it could be so sweet.

Four months after our wedding, we still had not taken a honeymoon and I was beginning to feel a bit uncomfortable about it. In July, however, we had both earned enough vacation time for a honeymoon getaway. I suggested we attend the convention of the Southern Federation of Syrian Lebanese American Clubs in Miami, Florida. Adelene didn't know that Lebanese Americans had conventions, much less a federation to organize them. She was a bit skeptical, to say the least. Truth be told, I think she thought I was crazy. After all, this was *our* honeymoon. Were we really going to spend it at a convention with a thousand people? I gulped hard and assured her she would have the time of her life.

For me and many others, the federation serves many functions.

First, it is a group of people of Syrian Lebanese heritage who come together to preserve the culture of our ancestors, meet people of similar backgrounds, and enjoy food and dance. The convention is also a way to network for business, as well as a giant debutant ball for singles. But most of all, it's an opportunity to reconnect with old friends, dance, and have fun.

Adelene agreed it might be fun. The road trip would give us some time alone before the convention. However, it took a few days for me to mention I had invited two of my brothers, Johnnie and Louis, to join us. She looked at me with a stare of disbelief that pierced my heart. Eventually, however, she agreed. Adelene and my family got along great. My brothers treated her as a sister, and she loved my entire tribe from the moment we got married. After seeing her side of the aisle at the wedding, I was actually a bit surprised she blended with my family so well.

We arrived at the convention and the lobby was filled with people. There were young people dressed to the nines everywhere, visiting, kissing, hugging, and even dancing—yes, dancing—in the lobby. Sitting in the middle of the lobby were several men playing the *darbuka*, an Arabic drum. People had formed a line and were dancing to the beat—it was the original line dance.

Adelene seemed to fit right in. Her personality was friendly and warm, and she was (and is) a beautiful woman. In fact, when we walked in, many heads turned to see the classic beauty on my arm. Her grace and charm captivated the crowd. I have to say I was a bit jealous.

The entire week is still etched in my memory, but two events stand out. The first occurred on the night we arrived, and the second when we were nearly ready to leave. The first night of a convention is usually one of the most fun. And with every evening event, there is always dancing. Everyone is renewing old friendships, forming new ones, and catching up on each other's lives. We always greeted each other by saying, "When did you get in?"

On the first night, the ballroom was filled to capacity. When we entered the room, I saw all the tables were nearly filled. Where were we going to find room for the four of us? I spotted a table in the center of the room and immediately went there. Adelene and my brothers followed dutifully. When we got there, I realized why the table had not been taken. A pillar next to the table blocked the view of the dance floor. My first thought was that we should find another spot, but upon further reflection I realized the pillar could be an asset. Turning adversity into triumph was always one of my skills.

I was jealous of the way all the men admired my beautiful Adelene, but I also found I had been remiss in informing many of the Lebanese women I had met at earlier conventions that I was now married. There was the ring on my finger, of course, but I knew there would be many questions. I realized I could use the pillar as a shield of sorts. On one side, I could entertain and adore my new bride. On the other side, I could gently inform those with whom I used to flirt so fondly that I was no longer on the market, so to speak.

My plan was not entirely foolproof. At one point, I was standing in front of the pillar and Adelene was sitting behind it with Johnnie. Angie, one of the girls I met the previous year called from the dance floor.

"Ralph! Ralph!"

Before responding, I looked behind me to make sure Adelene

was securely behind the pillar. She was talking to Johnnie. With the coast clear, I smiled and greeted Angie with a kiss on the cheek. She embraced me and told me how great it was to see me again. She said she had thought about me a lot during the past year and was glad I was there. I began to stutter, for I knew it was going to go downhill from here. I told Angie I had gotten married a few months earlier. All of a sudden, she began to cry hysterically.

"What? Are you kidding? *Married?!* You promised me you'd wait for me, Ralph! Why didn't you call and tell me?" she screamed for the entire convention to hear.

Well, that was all it took. From behind the pillar, she came! I felt my new bride's eyes searing into the back of my head. Angie and I had done little more than hold hands, but I knew it would be hard to convince Adelene of that now.

In her gracious style, Adelene introduced herself to the woman standing next to me.

"Hello," she said. "I am Adelene Abercia. And you are who?"

At this point, I wanted to dive behind the pillar myself. I didn't, though, and Adelene was as kind and wonderful as could be. I was confident in who I married, and that confidence has been confirmed every day of our lives. I wish the exchange with Angie was the only one of the night, but that would not be true. There were two or three others—though Adelene attests to a larger number—but each encounter ended miraculously with us all being friends. Believe it or not, we still see some of these same people at conventions to this day. That night brings laughter each time we reminisce.

The second event I remember well occurred on the final day of our stay. Each morning Adelene, Johnnie, Louis, and I had breakfast at the diner down the street from the hotel. The reason? It was ninety-nine cents and all you can eat. After breakfast, we returned to the hotel to attend meetings and other events for the day. Out of habit, we sat in the same booth each day for six days, and the same young lady waited on us. The only thing that changed was the seating arrangement. Over the six days, our waitress saw each one of us sitting next to Adelene. I am sure that a casual observer would have wondered what exactly was going on, for Adelene was very sweet and attentive to each one of us. I think Adelene played it up a little because she loved having the attention of three men. It was clear we were all taken by her, and none more than I.

As our waitress took our order on the last day, we noticed a confused look on her face. She hesitated and looked us each in the eye.

"I know this is none of my business," she said, "but which one of you gentlemen is married to this lady?"

Without a second of hesitation, all three of us raised our hands and answered, "I am!"

She didn't know what to say and just stood there for an awkward moment before we all burst into laughter.

TWO MONUMENTAL EVENTS

We undertook many more adventures during that marvelous trip. Not all of them were with my brothers or anyone else, of course, but those remembrances are just for me. Suffice it to say that Adelene and I finally had the honeymoon we hoped for. It was not typical, I know, but I never wanted a typical life, and neither did she. In some ways, our honeymoon helped to set the tone for the rest of our lives.

We always stayed close to our families, especially mine. After all, they were in Houston, there were a lot of them, and we never lived far apart. We also stayed close to the Lebanese community and attended many conventions over the years. In time, we even took our rightful place in the spotlight and served on the board of the Southern Federation. We each spent many hours as committee chairs and eventually served as Southern Federation presidents. This was a prestigious opportunity not only to participate, but to lead the Federation forward. It was also a way for us, as Americans, to enjoy our heritage and to pass that heritage along to the next generation.

Neither Adelene nor I were born in Lebanon, but we both

felt—and still feel—it is important for us and our children to have a sense of our ancestry and culture. We are all, to one degree or another, products of our past. It's important to understand the past if we are to understand ourselves and shape our futures.

Returning to Houston after our honeymoon, we fell into the routine of life. Most of us remember the extraordinary events of our lives and forget the more subtle ones. I suffer from the same affliction, but I do remember this particular period as being especially wonderful and rewarding. We were both working hard, making a good living, and learning to enjoy a touch of Houston society.

Adelene came by this honestly. After all, she and her family were steeped in the Fort Worth social scene. I had to work at it a little harder. I was used to working at parties rather than mingling. But I soon learned, with the help of my adoring wife, the fellowship of friends and the importance it plays in our lives. And so, we went on this way until two monumental events changed our lives forever. Of course, they occurred at nearly the same time.

I had been working successfully at the mortgage company, but always dreamed of practicing law. I suppose part of it was my upbringing. How could I spend so much time, effort, and money getting a JD and then not use it? It was like buying a shirt and then never wearing it. It just didn't seem right. I have to admit, I always wanted to be my own boss. Working for others was fine, but a tiny voice inside of me kept whispering I should go out on my own. I ignored it for as long as I could, but I finally relented. So, in the spring of 1954 I set in motion our first monumental event when I decided to open my own law practice.

I remember going home one night to announce my intentions to Adelene and get her reaction. I found her sipping lemonade at the kitchen table when I walked in. I hung my hat on the stand and rested my briefcase near the door before joining her.

"Adelene, I think it's time for me to start my own law practice," I said.

I think it was one of the few times in our lives when I caught her speechless. She slowly placed her glass of lemonade on the Formica tabletop and stared at me for a moment, her jaw slightly slack.

"Are you crazy, Ralph?" she finally said. "I'm going to give birth in a month, we have eighty-five dollars in the bank, and you want to start your law practice now?"

Thinking back, it may not have been perfect timing, but it never is. Sometimes a person just has to go with their gut, and that is what I did.

Our first child was our second monumental event. The birth of Sharon occurred exactly thirty-eight days after I opened the doors of my law practice. Sharon didn't want to come. When she was two weeks late, my mother-in-law gave Adelene castor oil to grease the skids, so to speak. *Castor oil?* I thought. *How strange!* But I didn't question it.

I also didn't question when Altus told me to take Adelene for a ride in the car and hit a lot of bumps. I simply did as I was told. I helped my very pregnant wife into the car, found an old road in Houston, and hit every pothole I could find. I think I hurt my back that night, but how could I complain when my wife and unborn baby were sitting in the front seat, doing just fine, and almost enjoying the ride?

Sharon finally came. I was so excited that day, I can't remember much besides being at the hospital with my family all around and feeling like I just won a sweepstakes. My God, she was beautiful, and she was mine. In those days, fathers were not allowed in the delivery room, so the first time I saw Sharon was in the arms of her mother in the recovery room.

I entered alone, with the voices of my brothers and sister still ringing in my ears. I froze just inside the door. It felt like the first time I entered St. Paul's Cathedral in London. Then the nurse motioned me over, and I beheld mother and child like I'd never seen it before—this was *my* wife and *my* child. I had a family of my own. I suppose everyone reacts to situations like this differently, but for me it was the proudest, most calming experience of my life. And although Adelene and I would be blessed with three more beautiful children in our lives, there is nothing like looking into the eyes of your own child for the first time.

Deep inside me arose an incredible sense of responsibility for this baby. I wanted to be there for her. I wanted her to know me; I wanted us to have a relationship. When Sharon looked back into my eyes with her finger pointed at me, I knew our relationship would be like no other in my life. There was a knowing in this little baby's gaze. I knew she would be a strong force in our lives, and I was right.

Adelene was hesitantly supportive of my new law practice. After looking for the best location to open an office, I found a very modest space downtown in the Citizens State Bank building. I was fortunate to be a few doors down from a well-known and successful law firm, Patterson and Patterson.

I secretly hoped to attract a client or two from them, although it would have been hard to mistake my office for theirs. When a client entered their firm, the huge maple double doors with gold hardware swung open wide to reveal a large waiting room with sofas, highbacked chairs, and an attractive receptionist behind a mahogany desk.

In stark contrast to the luxurious Patterson and Patterson, the single door to my law firm barely opened halfway before striking an unoccupied secretary's desk sitting on a concrete floor. This was also the case in my office. Clients had to enter sideways through a half-open door, as my desk and two chairs took up the majority of the room. It was the last available space in the building and the landlord was unable to lease it to most enterprises, which was why I got such a good deal on rent.

My practice was based on word of mouth, and of course I used my connections in the mortgage and title business. I think one or two of my first clients were actually destined for Patterson and Patterson but ended up in my meager surroundings. They were looking for legal assistance, so I obliged. Our offices were not plush, but our prices were extremely attractive. Client by client and case by case, both my practice and my reputation grew, and before I knew it, I had outgrown my cracker-box office and was looking for new space. I found it at 609 Fannin Street, prime real estate two blocks from the courthouse. I also found the indomitable Mrs. Ruth Martin, a force of character who would be with me for the next twenty-six years.

Over the years, Mrs. Martin and I grew together. A full twenty-eight years older than me, gray-haired, petite, and country through and through, she treated me like a son. I reciprocated by

THE HOUSTONIAN   PAGE 3

THESE ARE LAWYERS WE RECOMMEND

The purpose of this column is to name and recommend the good and ethical lawyers of Houston.

Those lawyers whom we considered to be shysters are never mentioned among the lawyers we recommend.

Fifty attorneys are recommended this week. There will be another 50 next week.

(If any lawyers who are paid subscribers are omitted from the following list, if they are qualified when their names should appear in alphabetical order, it is an oversight on our part, and we would appreciate their notifying us of that omission.)

We invite attorneys who are not regular readers to clip the subscription blank on the back page and become subscribers so they can read this newspaper every week. We also invite the above named attorneys to mail us their photographs and biographical sketches if we don't already have them. Thanks.)

Ralph Abercia.
Able & Graham.
James L. Abney.
Ben L. Adams, Jr.
Joe L. Allbritton.
Harry P. Allen.
R. G. Allen Jr.
Judge Harold Allison.
William Amaimo.
A. E. Amerman, Jr.
Dillon Anderson.
Wiley N. Anderson.
Jesse Andrews.
U. Stanley Ardoin.
Lawwrence Arnim.
Ed Arnold.
T. J. Arnold.
Louis S. Aselin.
Ed S. Atkinson.
M. J. Atlas.
Charles W. Austin.
D. H. Austin.
W. D. Avra.
Jack K. Ayer
Kenneth H. Aynesworth, Jr.
Aynesworth & Mann.
A. D. Azios.
Hector B. Azios.

R. G. ALLEN

RALPH ABERCIA

A. D. AZIOS

NEED ANY
BUSINESS CARDS?

The Houstonian article from the late 1950s or early 1960s
featured Ralph as one of the top lawyers in the city of Houston.

playing the part of her prodigal son. This smart woman was an incredible asset to my practice, and she protected me from many dangers I did not see.

As my clientele increased, I felt Mrs. Martin needed help, although she never asked for it. So, acting on my own instincts, I hired a young woman named Sherri as a receptionist. Disorganized, tardy, young, blond, and very well-endowed—everything Mrs. Martin was not. Needless to say, I hired her without any input from Mrs. Martin. At the time, I saw Sherri as the perfect person to greet our clients as they entered the office. It wasn't long before Mrs. Martin was in my office complaining and pointing out the error of my ways.

One morning I arrived at the office and, to my horror, found Mrs. Martin dressed in a tight sweater, a miniskirt, and go-go boots. A cheap blond wig sat precariously atop her head. I was speechless. Like a child who knew he broke the rules, I knew I was in trouble. I walked silently to my office. Mrs. Martin followed me closely, her breath practically on the back of my neck. I tried to ignore her as I fumbled through my briefcase. When I finally sat in my chair and looked up, I was frozen by Mrs. Martin's glare.

I asked if there was a problem, which elicited a sarcastic look and a tilt of her head. We sat in silence for what seemed like an eternity. Then Mrs. Martin sat forward in her chair and waved her bony finger at me.

"Come with me, Ralph. I want to show you something," she ordered.

I knew this was my office and my firm, but I also knew who ran it. So, like a schoolboy, I obediently stood and followed. In the reception area, I watched Mrs. Martin walk over to the far filing cabinet, bent over at the waist, and pulled out the bottom drawer. Her miniskirt barely covered her undergarments. I winced. She turned her head and pointed to her bottom.

"Ever since you hired that blond, this is what I see all day long. Either she goes, or I go!" she exclaimed.

Guess who was dismissed the next day? Sherri didn't take it well.

While my law practice was growing, so was my family. Adelene was pregnant with our second child. As with our first, the entire family, a mere twenty people, showed up at the hospital. I know my parents and Adelene's were waiting for a male heir, but they would have to wait a little longer. Sandra came into the world with purpose, but in a soft, demure way. She was petite, beautiful, and delicate with a force of strength; a giving nature permeated her being. Those attributes have continued to this day. She supports me in running the family business and is the glue that keeps us all together.

Our next baby was sweet little Mary Kathryn, the prettiest of babies. She had dark, soft curly hair with large hazel eyes and eyelashes that seemed to curl all the way to her forehead. Mary Kathryn was also our wise child, with an innate insight about a great many things. As she grew, her deep connection with God became apparent. Her intuition was almost empathic, and she became skilled at healing through herbs and homeopathic remedies. Her dreams were simple: to be a wife and a mother. Along with her many gifts, she retains a childlike innocence that makes her a joy to be around.

After having three beautiful girls who would give me great joy in life, we decided to have one more child. We were still looking for a male heir—a boy to carry on the family name. My father-in-law, John, was looking for the same thing.

My in-laws came down to Houston to help us about a month ahead of Sharon's birth. The day Sharon was born, my father-in-law, John, showed up with two dozen blue balloons, candy, and cigars. He was anticipating a boy. When Sharon showed up, he was a bit disappointed, but he passed out all the goodies anyway.

With sweet Sandra, the in-laws came down two weeks ahead to assist Adelene. That day at the hospital, John showed up with one dozen blue balloons and cigars, but no candy. I came running out.

"It's a girl!" I announced.

I could see the disappointment on his face, but he rose and congratulated me with a hug. For Big John, that was a true show of emotion. Then he passed out the balloons and cigars.

When the birth of our third child was upon us, our in-laws came down only a week ahead of time. John showed up at the hospital with nothing in his hands this time.

"This better be a boy," he said.

I came out for the third time with the same news.

"It's a girl."

John rose from the chair, shook my hand, and walked to the exit.

When we called Adelene's parents to announce there would be a fourth and final child, there was an awkward silence.

"Ralph, call us if it is a boy," John said.

Everything was different with this birth. The novelty of the firstborn had worn off and my siblings were all having children of their own. This time I took Adelene to the hospital alone. I lingered in the waiting room, paced up and down, prayed baby and mother would be healthy, and secretly hoped for a boy.

Sandra, Mary Kathryn, and Sharon Abercia one Easter Sunday at St. George Orthodox Church in Houston, Texas, in the early 1960s.

The baptism of Ralph Jr., at Ralph and Adelene's home in 1961. Ralph's father-in-law, John, was finally given the grandson he'd been waiting for.

The nurse came out and signaled for me to enter the room. I didn't ask the gender, for I wanted to see for myself. Adelene was sitting up in the bed and holding a tiny little baby. It had been an easy delivery for Adelene—the baby was only five pounds—and Adelene looked beautiful as always. As I walked closer, Adelene stared into my eyes.

"Meet your son, honey," she said.

I stopped dead in my tracks.

"A son? Is it true?" I asked.

"Yes," she replied. "A boy!"

I hugged my wife and our new son as if he were our first child. Then I reached over to the phone and called my father-in-law. I can still hear his gruff voice answering the phone.

"Yes?" he said.

"Pop," I told him, "we have a son."

His reply was short and simple.

"I am on my way."

We named him Ralph. He's not a true junior, though, for we gave him my father-in-law's middle name, Ferris. He was a beautiful baby with soft, blond, curly hair; fair skin; and large, hazel eyes. He was a sweet boy and so loving. I don't think his feet touched the ground for the first two years of his life. He was carried by everyone in the family. He was good-natured and very loving to his sisters; there wasn't a mean bone in him. As he grew, he brought laughter to our family with his antics.

With the birth of Ralph our family was complete. We went from being married and childless, exploring our social life, to a family of six in little more than seven years. During the same period, I grew my law practice from a fledgling business into something that sustained us all and allowed Adelene to focus exclusively on our children. Full-time motherhood is not as popular an avocation these days, but she was happy to undertake it. I wish all families had the option of considering it. Too many have no choice but to outsource the raising of their children to others.

I even found time to develop a piece of property or two along the way. But for all my efforts and success in law and real estate, my greatest joys in life have come from my family, my faith, and my life in a country that allowed me opportunity. I went from a barefoot street urchin desperately searching for a lost penny in the grass to a man with a loving wife and four magnificent children, each with gifts far superior to my own. Money comes and goes, fortunes can be made and lost, but the measure of a man's wealth is in his character and in what he leaves behind.

My faith has given me both the strength and the tenderness to identify what is needed and then to do it. My family, including my extended Lebanese family, has brought joy and fellowship into my life beyond anything I could ever repay. Finally, my country has nurtured and protected me all my life. And although I fear for her very existence at times, I am continually awed by her grandeur—by this grand experiment called America—and wish others would take the time to see her beauty and compassion.

FATHER JOHN

The siren is screaming in my ears so loud it hurts. The ambulance driver is going slowly, which means that I must be a high-risk case. I agreed to be transported by a special intensive care unit to the medical center for my pacemaker operation, but now I am wondering if I made the right decision.

Sharon is with me for the ride. She looks worried; her eyes are welling up with tears. They told me if my heart rate dropped too low during the drive, they would have to perform emergency surgery in the ambulance. That's a risky affair. I spy the EMT, who has a laser-like focus on the monitors in front of him. I can feel my strength start to wane, then my vision begins to narrow. There is perspiration on my forehead, and I know I must be clammy all over.

I watch Sharon say something to me, but I can't hear her. Perhaps my hearing has gone. The EMT is also looking down at me. There is concern on his face, and it seems like he's trying to elbow my dear Sharon out of the way. Good luck. I fully expect him to produce some high-tech medical pack, tear it open, extract a scalpel, and start sawing, but he doesn't.

Instead, he inserts a stethoscope in his ears and places the cold disc on my chest. I can't believe he can hear anything for the screeching of the siren, but it appears he can. After a moment he wraps the stethoscope around his neck and whispers something into my daughter's ear. She looks relieved, which makes me feel better. Suddenly I realize I am better; my vision is clearer, and the nausea is going away. We're backing up now. We must be at the Houston Medical Center. I've almost made it.

I see one unfamiliar face after another looking down at me as I'm wheeled toward the operating room. An oxygen mask covers my mouth and nose. We clear another set of doors, and I feel the temperature drop. We must have arrived in the operating room. Everyone is wearing masks. A pair of eyes looks down at me, and I think they are smiling. I hear someone ask me to count backward from a hundred. I only get to ninety-seven before darkness closes in.

I can see the tops of the buildings through the fog on the horizon. I can almost smell the city air, but something is amiss. When I blink my eyes, the buildings and fog are gone—or, I should say, they are only a picture on the wall. I look out the window to my right and see trees swaying in the wind. I want to open it, but I can't get it to work. Sharon is clasping my wrists to keep me from pounding on the glass. I stop for a moment and look around. I realize I must be in the hospital recovery room. Part of my mind knows these hallucinations are an unintended reaction to the anesthesia, but the other part desires to believe the dreams are real and longs to go back to my home on North Main.

I look down and see bare feet covered with dust. My pants are too short. I look up and see my brother Johnnie in the distance. He is waving at me to come with him. He looks the way he did as a kid. I clutch a loaf of my mother's bread to my chest. It's the last one I have, and I want to sell it before running off to meet my brother, but I feel someone pulling it from me. I suddenly feel angry.

"Let go of it, Dad," I hear my daughter say.

"Why do you want it?" I yell at her.

"Why do *you* want it, Dad?" she yells back.

I look down and realize we're playing tug-of-war with my urine bag, and it is spilling all over me.

"Dad, *please* let go. You are in the hospital."

I look around and see she's right. *What am I doing and where did Johnnie go?* I look in the distance, but all I see is the picture on the wall. I stare at it for a little while, and then let my eyes drop. I see something old and familiar. A glint from a piece of metal. I focus and there in the corner, wedged against the baseboard is a single copper penny. I remember the ecstasy of finding a lost penny in the grass many years ago on Freeman Street.

I ask Sharon to retrieve the penny and she does. She holds it up to the light and inspects it.

"Dad, it's only a penny," she sounds disappointed.

"Only a penny?" I exclaim. "My sweet daughter, it was pennies that kept my family alive."

Suddenly, I see Johnnie again.

"Johnnie, wait!" I cry out to him.

I let go of the loaf of bread. I think it falls to the ground. I look up and see Johnnie in the distance. He waves again before turning and trotting off into the tunnel we both hate so much. I wave as he turns to leave, and I yell goodbye as loud as I can. I hope he can hear me, but I doubt it. I'll have to catch up with him later.

I feel my daughter's hand on my forehead as I sink onto the bed. My head rests on the pillows, and I hear the soft coo of Sharon's voice as she does her best to soothe me. It's working, and now I know without a doubt that I am in my hospital room just before I drift off to sleep.

The next morning, I awake to the sound of commotion in my room, which is filled with my family. The doctors are taking questions from them. They explain I need rest and they must try and keep the room quiet. I do my part and close my eyes.

I try to hold my eyelids closed, but they won't stay that way. I don't want to sleep, even though I know I should. When I open my eyes, I see all the reasons I want to stay awake: my family. The sight of them warms my heart. They are whispering and trying to keep it down, but the room is anything but quiet. Quiet is simply not possible for us. I understand this and am happy for it.

The doctors operated and placed a pacemaker in my chest. I'm feeling better now. It's amazing how good you can feel when your heart is beating properly and your blood is being oxygenated. I don't need to see the monitor to know my heart is doing its work.

Being in a hospital room is not a new experience for me. I've had cancer three times and survived each one. Those events included eight operations—five on my neck (for my throat); two for my thyroid; and one on my stomach. However, this is the first time I've been hospitalized for a heart condition. I can't help but take a long look at my sister Juliette and remember her time in the hospital. I still think she had a harder time than I ever have.

I watch as my children stand in a semicircle and debate about some unknown topic. They're all in their fifties now, but I still see them as kids—a parent's perspective. Sharon, Sandra, and Mary Kathryn are all talking at the same time, and Ralph is trying to listen to all of them. I've seen this scene more times than I can remember. I know he wants to say something, but he can't get a word in edgewise. It won't be long before he rolls his eyes in frustration and finds another group to talk to.

My children's children are also in the room with us. By some coincidence, all my children ended up having two kids. The eight of them are grouped together. Bianca, Sandra's oldest, is carrying young Gabriel, Ralph's four-year-old, on her hip. It reminds me of when Ralph's sisters carried him when he was just a toddler. My brothers, less Johnnie, are also in the room, as is my dear sister Juliette.

Suddenly everyone is looking toward the door. I assume one of the doctors is here to examine me again. The mass of humanity parts. Instead of a white-smocked individual, a man in a black coat enters the room. I soon see the white collar and recognize Father John from our church, St. George. I'm honored he has taken the time to come visit me.

Father John knows our family well. We're all Orthodox, and we all love him, despite the fact that he is from Pittsburgh and is a Steelers fan. He approaches my bedside, and everyone fills in behind and around him. It's hard for me to explain the feeling of compassion and love surrounding us. We talk for a while, and he tells me how concerned everyone at church has been. This is comforting to me, as I love the people of Saint George and believe in the healing power of prayer. My family helped found Saint George, and we have served the church every day of our lives.

I spy Adelene sitting at my side and realize how blessed my life has been. I have often wondered why I was saved from death or serious injury during World War II when so many others were not. I can only reconcile this through my faith in God and his son Jesus Christ. Perhaps my life was meant to serve another purpose. And perhaps that purpose was to serve God and all the people in this room.

I awake to a new feeling of being alive. My body seems to have accepted the pacemaker with little objection. I've always been able to adapt quickly. At around 11 a.m., my electrophysiologist comes into the hospital room. My children and Adelene are still with me. The doctor tells us the pacemaker in my chest is a St. Jude pacemaker. This makes me happy, as I served on the St. Jude Children's Hospital Board for many years.

"Great," I tell the doctor. "It's a great omen to have St. Jude in my chest."

"It is the best, Ralph. It has a fifteen-year battery," he adds.

For some reason that statement sticks in my mind.

"Fifteen years?" I question. "Is that all?"

I can see the confusion on the doctor's face. I'm sure he thought he was giving me good news. After all, I am eighty-nine years old. He quickly recovers and laughs out loud.

"Ralph, I will put a new battery in when you turn 100 whether you need it or not," he announces.

Believe it or not, that statement provides me with a sense of relief, for I know I will be here to receive my new pacemaker. And I know my family will be with me.

EPILOGUE

In the spring of 2011, I traveled with my parents to Washington, D.C., for the rededication of the Kahlil Gibran Memorial. They were always happy to have me attend.

"Sharon, this will be your legacy before long," they would tell me.

My mother, Adelene, was an integral part of the original dedication in 1982, along with President George H.W. Bush and other dignitaries. The grounds had been left unkept for quite some time, and now the next generation of Lebanese had come together to re-beautify and rededicate Serenity Park on Embassy Row. The weekend was filled with fabulous events and celebrations, including a cocktail party at the Lebanese embassy, press conferences at the House of Representatives, and the rededication ceremony in the park.

The first press conference was held in congressional chambers and hosted on behalf of the White House. The chief of staff was there representing the president of the United States. He welcomed our group and answered questions on US policy. Several other dignitaries spoke as well. It was very exciting.

My parents and I were sitting at the back of the hall. My father got up to go outside for a few minutes. We didn't notice how long he was gone—or even if he had returned—because we were listening so intently. James Zogby, author of *Arab Voices*, approached the podium and announced there would be one more speaker who would give the closing remarks. I looked up and saw someone who looked remarkably like my father. Then I looked over to the chair next to my mother. It was empty. I looked back to the podium and thought, *Is that Dad standing in front?*

Although it wasn't part of the agenda, my father had been chosen to say a few words. I was not surprised. His leadership in the Lebanese community and the Orthodox Church had, over the years, reached national prominence. His message was simple and clear: devotion to our country, responsibility to stand up for our beliefs as Americans, and the importance of opening our hearts to help others and serving as an example for all.

As he came back to join my mother and me, we beamed with pride. Even at eighty-nine, he still conveys his message of God, family, and country in an eloquent manner. It is a message for all ages.

Dad's talent as an orator became evident during his days as a trial attorney. He had a reputation for closing arguments that were both powerful and mesmerizing. He had a silver tongue. Most of Dad's clients were poor minorities. He was their defender. He felt everyone should be given a fair chance. He and his brother Johnnie, my godfather, represented many of their clients for free or on a contingency basis.

Dad did well in his law practice, but commercial real estate was his love, and that is where he truly excelled. There was something about land and development that made Dad happy. Owning property gave him security. Numbers were another one of his talents. He could add, divide, multiply, or get a percentage faster than a calculator. He always said using your brain keeps it young and active.

He never stops. Work is and always has been his form of relaxation. His wife and children have encouraged him to retire many times.

"Retire?!" he would yell out. "What do you want me to do—go home, sit in a rocker, and waste away? I have too much to do."

He continues to see himself as a young man with a lot of living and learning left to do. One of the most intriguing characteristics of my father is how he is not afraid to take risks and doesn't think he is too old to start something new. He can see an opportunity in a business, and he is willing to take it on. Some ventures have been successful, while others have failed miserably. He chalked the failures up to experience and never dwelled on the negative. He would pass along his successes to a family member and move on to the next project.

Dad served on many boards and won many awards. He would be upset with me if I mentioned them here, for he feels there is always someone who has done more and is more deserving. I will say, however, that the Orthodox Church holds a special place in his heart and serving as the president of the National Board of the Orthodox Church and the president of St. Ignatius of Antioch meant a great deal to him. It gave him such pride to spread Orthodoxy throughout the United States; to raise money to fund camps for children and orphanages in South America and Lebanon; and to build churches in places that had never heard of Orthodoxy.

My father has always been drawn to music and dance; perhaps it is his way of celebrating life. There is a rhythm, a beat, to everything we humans do, and if you can feel that rhythm and learn to embrace it, you will enjoy life all the more. I know this is true, and I am eternally grateful Dad took the time to impart this simple fact to my siblings and me.

For years now I have watched my father at home, at work, and at church. He is the same man in all these places. He is always positive and encouraging, one of his most endearing qualities. Whenever I would come home sad, depressed, or feeling sorry for myself, he would always be there with kindness, encouragement, and love—as well as a constant reminder that I am in charge of my own future and my own happiness. I didn't always want to hear him, but I knew it was true.

I was always amazed by his attitude. No matter how rough things got, he never played the part of the victim. When life happens, it's just life. You haven't been singled out because life happens to everyone. It is what you do with life that counts.

"Be strong. Face life head on and figure out a way to make it happen!" Dad would say to me. Then he would kiss me on the forehead and say, "If you need my help, I am here."

I have watched this man win and lose fortunes and never bat an eye in the process. Perhaps it is true what Rudyard Kipling said:

> *If you can meet with Triumph and Disaster*
> *And treat those two impostors just the same . . .*
> *If you can make one heap of all your winnings*
> *And risk it on one turn of pitch-and-toss,*
> *And lose, and start again at your beginnings*

And never breathe a word about your loss . . .
Yours is the Earth and everything that's in it,
And—which is more—you'll be a Man, my son!

The older I get, the more I realize the virtue and value of my father, for he is truly the greatest man I have known. I can hear him say, "Why do you say that about me? You're making too big a deal of it. I am just a man doing what I am supposed to be doing."

Oh, how I wish more men were just doing what they are supposed to be doing. The world would be a better place.

—Sharon Aberica

MORE PHOTOS

Tofie and Libbie Abercia on their wedding day in 1921 in Houston, Texas. These were different times—Libbie was only fourteen years old.

Johnnie, Ralph, and William, the "Three Musketeers," likely of high school age, at their home on Freeman.

William Faour, Ralph's best friend and uncle, taught him everything he needed to know about being a salesman and navigating life. William is in his twenties in this photo.

Ralph being honored as a distinguished veteran at a Houston Texans football game in 2019.

Abercia family photo in Houston around the early 1940s. Standing in the back row are Kenneth Faorf (cousin), Johnnie, and Ralph. Juliette is kneeling in the middle. In the front row are Louis, Jack, and George.

Likely in the 1990s, the Abercia siblings as adults: back row, Ralph, George, Johnnie; front row, Jack, Juliette, Louis.

Photographer credit: Sofia van der Dys

ABOUT THE AUTHORS

Married couple John Evans and Sharon Abercia met in a chance encounter after both attended a business meeting twelve years ago.

They spent the first year and a half of their relationship writing *Only a Penny*, the story of a Lebanese immigrant family, her father's, who crawled out of profound poverty to achieve national prominence. Sharon's father, Ralph Abercia, is a native Houstonian, who is a member of the Greatest Generation, and just turned 100 years old in August 2023.

Sharon has a BS in marketing and advertising from the University of Texas in Austin and is the founder of The Monarch PR Group. After leaving college, Sharon had a successful modeling career and owned The Ben Shaw Modeling and Talent

Agency. Sharon also spent several years in the oil and gas business as founder of Tri-Coastal Energy Partners. Sharon's hobbies are writing and collecting art. She is also an officer/board member of several local and national organizations. She is involved in both local and national politics and also contributes to numerous charities. Sharon is very committed to her Lebanese community locally and nationally, as well as St. George Orthodox Christian Church and the Ladies of Houston Charity.

John has a BS in chemical engineering and an MBA in finance. He also holds a Professional Engineer License in the State of Texas. He attended the Naval Academy, the University of Colorado, and the University of New Orleans. John was a scholarship athlete in tennis at the University of Colorado and the Naval Academy. John currently works with TPC Group. His hobbies are sculpting and writing, and he also loves rare books and Middle Eastern poetry. In fact, he has a collection that was his grandfather's. In January of 2024, John had an unveiling of his latest sculpture, "Passion," a near life-size expression of an Arabic dancer.

Sharon and John reside in Houston, Texas, and have four beautiful adult children of whom they are very proud.

www.ingramcontent.com/pod-product-compliance
Lightning Source LLC
Chambersburg PA
CBHW060523080526
44586CB00012B/584